Lifelines

BG Stanley

Foreword by Homer Overstreet, Jr.

Lifelines © 2011 BG Stanley
First Edition
All rights reserved.

"The scripture quotations contained herein are from the New Revised Standard Version Bible (NRSV), Copyright © 1989 by the Division of Christian Education of the National Council of the Churches of Christ in the U.S.A. Used by permission. All rights reserved."

Scripture from the Rainbow Study Bible: Scripture taken from Holy Bible, New International Version (NIV) Copyright © 1973, 1978, 1984 by International Bible Society. Used by permission of Zondervan Publishing House. All rights reserved.

Job 42:5 Reprinted from TANAKH: The Holy Sriptures: The NEW JPS TRANSLATION TO THE TRADITIONAL HEBREW TEXT, 1985 by The Jewish Publication Society, with the permission of the publisher.

Permission to copy or reproduce material from this book can be obtained from the author: brim4peace@gmail.com

Cover Design BG Stanley and Xlibris
Hands: Curtis, Regina and MaKenzie Anderson
Heart on Cover by Dreamstime/Robert Elfferich
Layout of Images: Xlibris

Copyright © 2012 by BG Stanley. 581595

ISBN: Softcover   978-1-4500-1778-7

All rights reserved. No part of this book may be reproduced or transmitted in any form or by any means, electronic or mechanical, including photocopying, recording, or by any information storage and retrieval system, without permission in writing from the copyright owner.

Print information available on the last page.

To order additional copies of this book, contact:
Xlibris
1-888-795-4274
www.Xlibris.com
Orders@Xlibris.com

Acknowledgments

This book is fondly dedicated to my parents, the late Lawyer Stanley, Sr. and the late, Lena M. Montgomery-Stanley, the most kind and caring people I have ever known. They were both humanitarians, true givers of the heart, and so warm and accepting of others. I am proud to have had such wonderful parents. They gave me life, but more importantly, they taught me how to live my best life; to be giving, loving, kind, helpful, confident, genuine, and to be giving, loving, kind, helpful, confident, genuine, loyal and courageous. I will always honor them by my life and service.

I also dedicate this book to my brothers and sisters, Linda, Rickey, Connie, Calvin, Regina and Tony, my dear nieces and nephews, and my goddaughters, Genesha and Melissa. A special graciousness goes to my youngest sister and friend, Regina Anderson, (Ladybird), who has always been my most avid listener and critic even on her busiest days. She compelled me to write this book in order to share these words with the world. She believed that my poetry was about life and that these poems would inspire, uplift, and encourage anyone who read them.

This book is also dedicated to all of my friends and supporters who patiently listened to and read these poems: my eldest sister, the late Dorothy Stanley-Belcher, Ayo Jones, Janet Billups, Kathy Stanley, Pauline Brown, Aunt Ada Bailey, Mother Martha Ellis, Mother Janie Davis, Flore Coppee, Dolores Yilibuw, Dell Rowe, Delmarie Cook, Linda Ross, Christine Long, June Lowe, Martha Dunlap, Gwenelyn Lockhart, Homer Overstreet, Allen Vanderhorst, Devon Marion, Renee Lawrence, Brenda Zachery, Sonia Brown, my wonderful mentor, Norma, and my dear friend, Dianne Marion (Sis), who listened, read, and allowed me to use her computer to complete this book and all my other projects. A special thanks to Polly Charette for helping me get to this place. And above all, I thank God for every gift, every revelation, and every inspiration.

Table of Contents

Foreword by Homer Overstreet, Jr. 7
Introduction 8

I. Connected 9
    Connected 10
    Born Again (Miraculous) 11

II. Breath of Life 12
    Healing the wounds of abuse 13
    One Breath 14
    I Want To Live 15
    Lifesavers 16
    Sweet 16 17
    No Caged Birds 18
    Sticks and Stones 19
    Remembrance 20
    You tore a hole in my soul 21
    I was once the woman 22
    I walked away 23
    Celebrating You 24

III. Storylines 25
    Tell your story 26
    Somebody's Story 27
    Somebody took care of that baby 29
    Tug-of-War 30
    To the mother who wanted me 31
    Felony 32
    Relapse 33
    High 33
    The Prize within 34
    Figure skating for the gold 35
    You don't know my story 36

IV. Lifelines 37
    Wooden floors 38
    Growth Spurts 39
    Lifeline 41
    Lines 42
    Life's beauty marks 43

V. Children 44
    Children 45
    It still takes a Village 46
    Families Build Bridges 50

VI. Love lines 51
    I Want a Forever Love 52
    Seeking Hearts 53
    Love is Magical 54
    Love Grows 54

  Promise 55

VII. Living Faith ("Faith, Hope and Love, these three . . ." NRSV) 56
  Answering Moses 57
  "The just shall live by faith" 60
  I Am 60
  Faith in the desert 61
  Worship begins within 62
  I'll be an instrument for thee 62
  Untitled 63
  In Your Presence 64
  Reflection 65
  Hope 66
  Survival 67
  Samaritans 68
  The Best Gift 69

VIII. Signs of Life 70
  Giving Life 71
  When somebody loves you 72
  What's important to you? 73

IX. The Magnificence of Life 76
  Our Lives can change with every breath 77
  The Magnificence of Life 78
  Bless this sanctuary called Earth 79

X. The Colors of America 80
  The Colors of America 82
  Ignorance 85
  The King's Dream 86
  Rainbow 87
  We are all People 88

XI. Because of You 89
  Letter of Thanks 90
  Because of You 91
  My brother does not know me anymore 92
  Tres Madres lloronanda (three mothers weeping) 93
  For all the black women in the struggle 94
  Born Free 95
  You stood for us 96
  Waiting 97
  Standing 98
  They saw it coming 99

XII. Timelines: From Breath to Breath 100
  Kiss the Living 101
  Save the Date 102
  The Living and the Dead 103
  Love me now 104
  Mother-[muhth-er] 105
  Cemeteries 106
  Listen to her heart 107
   Credits 109

FOREWORD

I enjoyed reading BG Stanley's book of prose and poetry which was written over several decades of her life.

The book celebrates life, family, children, love, joys, and sorrows.

It is a powerful book with many deep meanings.

Homer Overstreet, Jr.

Poet

Introduction

This is Lifelines. It pulsates. It speaks. It stirs the thoughts; opening the eyes to see beyond the ordinary and embrace the things in life that matter most. Lifelines is a book that you will read again and again. In these pages, you will find many relevant experiences, such depth of thought, and a masterful conveyance of the spoken word. This book will move you because it is inspired by people, from babies to centenarians. It was written from the heart and soul of life to show the rich meanings found in our everyday lives. It elevates the joys, the sorrows, birth, love, the magnificence of life, social issues, struggles, tragedies and triumphs to show the interconnectedness of our humanity. The voices of the past also echo in these pages reminding us of lessons and progress, "Lest we forget."

Lifelines will challenge your thinking, motivate your spirit, and uplift your heart because it is in tune with the rhythms of life itself. It connects. These contemplative chords of prose and poetry are profoundly powerful.

This book is captivating. Read it from the beginning to the ending. Enjoy the magnificent pictures that accompany these memorable words compiled into twelve chapters. The book opens up with 'Connected', which calls on all of us to speak out for one another. "If all the voices of all the people were raised. . . " Chapter Two, The Breath of Life, was inspired during my volunteer service with women and children displaced by Domestic Violence. I have attempted to respectfully capture their feelings, their pain, and their resilience. The advocates are also honored in a poem entitled, Lifesavers. Chapter Three, Storylines, tells real stories about real lives, our 'Once upon a time.' In chapter four, several symbols of Lifelines are unveiled. It is followed by a playful poem on Children, the treasures of life. Love lines is a splendid chapter on love. Chapter Seven taps into our faith and the hope which sustains and grounds us through our valley experiences. Chapter Ten, the 'Colors of America,' celebrates the richness of our diversity. Chapter Eleven is dedicated to those whose legacies have empowered us and helped transform the world. Chapter Twelve eloquently speaks of our sorrows and lost loves, our cherished memories of them and the fragrance that they leave. It reminds us to 'Kiss the Living.'

This is Lifelines. This is a book about life from me, a poet, who has been divinely inspired by some of my own life experiences, people that I have met or heard about, and their stories. It was written from my heart, soul, and mind. It is bursting with messages and rich meanings found in the heartbeats of life for it captures the rhythms of real lives from its opening crescendo to its closing melody.

Connected

One of my favorite quotes is one made by Dr. Martin Luther King, Jr. He said, "We are all interrelated and interconnected, tied up in a single garment of destiny. Whatever affects one directly, affects all indirectly. . ."

This first poem attempts to capture our need to support one another as we strive to maintain a humane society.

In remembrance of all the victims of hate crimes in America and all over the world.

Connected

If all the voices of all the people were raised
to speak out against injustice
the violence of our days,
exploitation, abuse, indignities,
against women in the world would end,
if all the voices cried, STOP,
no more 'human sin'!
For violence against one another
tears the world apart
and where there is no compassion,
no love is in your heart.
If no-one stood by silent
while others inflicted pain
upon children and the innocent
to join a violent gang;
If all the people cried at once
against racism, sexism and hate,
discrimination and slurs would cease
and tensions would abate.
If all the voices of all the people
spoke for justice and human rights
then maybe we could have peace in this world
and end these 'senseless' fights;
then maybe everyone could prosper,
and every baby be fed
if all the people spoke against greed and corruption
so that everyone could move ahead.
If all the voices of all the people
spoke against terrorism and tyranny,
then maybe the world will know,
the strength in unity.
If all the voices of all the people,
did not stand silently by
as drugs consumed our children
driving crime and death rates high——
If all the people understood
our interconnectedness,
then no one could stand by silent
while others are treated less.
If all the voices of all the people
against inhumanity was raised,
then the world would be better for all of us,
and God would surely be praised.

Born Again (Miraculous)

*For it was you who formed my inward parts; you knit me together in my mother's womb.
I praise you because I am fearfully and wondrously made. . . Psalms 139: 13 (NRSV)*

From a tiny cell, I became,
before I even had a name,
I had a heart that beat like a drum,
I could blink my eyes and suck my thumb.
I am so marvelously and wondrously made!

In the depths of my mother's womb,
in the darkness there was light,
for eyes sprang forth, and gave me sight.
Kidneys formed so that urine could flow,
bones and marrow began to grow.
I am so marvelously and wondrously made!

Even in her waters I could breathe,
her vessels supplying my every need,
in my mothers womb warm and soft,
I could drink; I could feed.
And my liver grew, my bowels too.
I am so marvelously and wondrously made!

And then at an appointed time
my body turned itself to find
the perfect spot for comfort and nesting
'til I came forth to be a blessing;
a joy to my father and mother kind
and *evidence* of God divine.
I am so marvelously and wondrously made!

Since my birth was a miracle in the earth
I too must give some value some worth
to others who came forth like me
but struggle to live and be free.
For those who hurt and are wounded and sad,
God formed my hands to make them glad
by giving and doing what good I can
for any child, woman, or man.
So let me not neglect the gift in me
endowed before I came to be,
Let me not sit in apathy
and insult the Creator who 'created' me.
Let me serve, let me give
so that I may truly live
my full life
that was meant to be
when a miraculous God formed me,
Miraculously!

Healing the Wounds of Abuse

All I want is to be whole,
from my head to my heart
to my soul.
All I want is to be free
from these bruises and scars
outwardly and
inwardly
that hinder me.
I am crying out,
I want to shout,
Let me out, let me out,
Let me be, Let me be,
Free!
Heal these wounds,
mend my head,
pick up the pieces of my broken heart,
I need a new start,
I need a full life,
I can no longer be
a battered wife,
a battered friend,
I need this nightmare to come to an end
right now!
I need to be free to be me.
No more fears and fists, no more harsh words,
I will be as free as an uncaged bird,
you'll see.
'Thank you for supporting me.'

One Breath

In one breath you say that you love me,
in the next, you take it away,
with violence, abuse and pain,
then you promise me a better day.

In one breath I was born,
not knowing that one day
I would meet a charming person
who would 'take my breath away.'

'Take my breath away'
with passion and intimacy,
then 'take my breath away'
controlling and destroying me.

But before I gave up my last breath
to the one who once 'took it away,'
I took courage and I left
before he took
          my breath
              away.

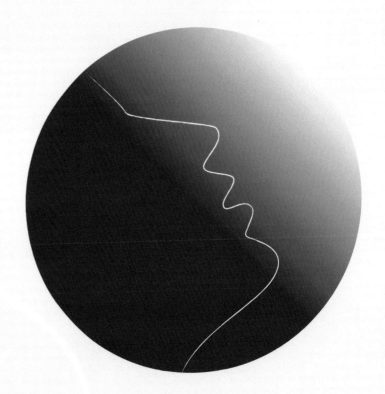

I Want To Live

I can't breathe
and I am afraid to walk too hard
on the floor
and wake you from your sleep
to be slapped and kicked and punched
for disturbing your rest,
even with our baby growing inside
my womb.
I can't breathe, even though the
words I want to say linger on my
swollen lips.
I dare not even whisper.
Silence and violence rule
my life
and I can't
breathe,
I can't scream,
I can't dream.
Everything I do is wrong,
every word is wrong,
every effort is wrong.
I can't breathe,
I can't even sing a song.
My hands are numb
as I sit watching the ticking clock
second by second
sucking the life out of me.
I can't breathe
because of the grasp of your angry
hands around my neck.
Hear my pounding heart
suffocating like a diver
whose tank is empty;
my chest ready to burst
racing to the surface,
fleeing death
because
I can't breathe —
but,
    I want to live!

Lifesavers

This poem is dedicated to all of the supporters and volunteers that aid the victims of domestic violence and abuse by providing shelter, legal aid, security, counseling, medical assistance and a renewed breath of life. You are LIFESAVERS.

He yelled because I forgot
to purchase his cigarettes from the mart.
Then he hit me and made me cry,
but I hid my blackened eye
from my family and from my friends;
he apologized sweetly,
but he hit me again.
He hit me because I had to work late,
cursing, yelling, fierce debates
and even though I tried to do everything right,
he always found a reason to fight.
He hit me because I did not make the bed,
but I was trying to make sure that the children were fed.
He'd hit me if his shirt was torn,
if the children were noisy,
if I didn't cook corn.
He'd rant and rave and push and yell,
it was a nightmare, a living hell.
He hit me until I lay down,
and when I began to drown
a hand reached out and pulled me in
so that my life could begin again.
Thank you for setting me free,
for being there to rescue me.

Sweet 16

Sweet sixteen, what's that on your pretty face,
underneath those pretty lashes I see,
a bruise that your make-up can't cover up,
did your boyfriend beat you up?
Did he hit you and make you cry
then said that you were the reason why
he was mad, and things weren't right,
you are the cause for the fight,—
"If you loved him then you'd stay."
He hits you, but he loves you anyway?

Well, let me tell you girl,
it's not true,
If he really, really loved you
he would treat you like a queen
not tear down your self-esteem
nor control your free voice,
taking away your rights, your choice,
where to go, who to see;
he would freely let you be
YOU!

He would not inflict hurt and pain
and call you all those obscene names.
Listen to what I'm telling you girl;
there is true love in this world.
Love is kind and love is real,
love is more than a passing thrill,
love lifts up and love makes strong,
abuse has to STOP,
but love goes on.
So don't let anyone take your 'life' away,
You have a future, and it starts today.

No Caged Birds

For women and girls in every continent of the world who are not free and who are not treated humanely and justly.

No woman should be caged
they should all be free,
to speak, to choose, to go,
to be.
Let them all be as free as birds
against a summer sky,
like a butterfly
floating by —
with angels wings
let them take flight
give them their voice
give them their right.
Give them what has been taken away,
Give them their life; let them have their say,
You cannot own their freedom anyway.

You who bind them can never be free
until you relinquish their liberty.
You are not, if they cannot be,
So let them be, let them be,
Free!

Sticks and Stones

"Sticks and stones may break my bones, but words can never hurt me;"
a rhyme we used to playfully say, to make the pain go away—
Though broken bones break and heal
the pain of words linger still
piercing my heart everyday
the mean words you constantly say.
You call me names, you tear me down,
You turn my mind upside down.
I cannot take another word
for everything that I have heard
from your mouth
vicious and mean,
apologies can't redeem.
So please don't think the harsh words you say
vanish and just go away,
for words have power and words have life,
words bring peace, or words bring strife.
So if hurtful words are all you have to say
then I must leave and go away,
where I can mend, where I can heal,
where I can find a place to kneel
and be comforted from the words you said
which still echo in my head.
I need a place to be revived,
a place where I can feel alive,
I need to hear healing words
to mend my soul from those I've heard.
People who care, 'call me by name'
saying that I am not to blame
for the damage that you have done
for the scars, every one.
Though cruel words may not break bones
they hurt as much as sticks and stones,
 They wound so deeply; they linger on.

* * * * * * *

Today I no longer believe what I have heard
because abuse does not have the final word.

Remembrance

All you wanted was to be loved.
All you wanted was life.
All you wanted was freedom
from abuse and strife.
But the abuse became more violent
until your voice was silent
and all of us who are gathered here
still hold the memories of you dear.
A beautiful life soon taken away
teaches us all a better way,
a better way to help those who are here
living in abuse, living in fear.
The memory of your life will not cease
until all can have a life of peace;
away from harm, away from pain,
until all can be whole again.
We will remember you
and what you went through,
but we will take note of your beautiful life
for you were more than a battered wife,
— a human being
with immeasurable worth;
your death gives life; your death gives birth
to laws and acts and legislation,
to shelters and volunteers,
so we shine this light to remember You,
each day, each moment, each year.

You tore a hole in my soul

You tore a hole in my soul
when you pierced me in my side
and I almost died
like the crucified
one.
But I wanted to live;
so I got down off the cross
that you nailed me to
bleeding, torn and sad,
I got off that cross
and I never looked back
to that Gethsemane
I once had.
I looked forward to a new day
because Jesus came my way;
touched my head,
healed my heart,
closed the wound in my side,
and <u>kissed</u> my nail pierced hands.
Then I knew what it meant to be
resurrected to life.
This is the story
of a battered wife.

For all of my church sisters who were encouraged to stay…

I was once the Woman

I was once the woman who prayed and stayed
and endured the fights
every night.
I was once the woman
who feared being alone
standing on my own.
I was once the woman who
though beaten and bruised
refused
to leave;
who believed
that tomorrow
would end my sorrow
because he said,
"I LOVE YOU."
I was once the woman
he sometimes treated like a queen
after tearing down
my self-esteem.
I was once the woman
who kept going back
despite the abuse,
the verbal attacks,
trying to do everything
to keep peace,
but the abuse did not stop,
instead, it increased.
I was once the woman
of whom people would say,
"Why does she take it?"
"Why does she stay?"
There are so many reasons
why we stay,
sometimes believing,
it will just go away.
So I continued to be the woman
who lived in silence
with domestic violence;
the woman who passed you by
excusing the blackened eye
the broken arm and heart—
Today I am the woman,
who has a new start,
because,
I was once the woman who tried to believe
until I realized,
that in order to live,
I needed to leave.
I was once the woman . . .

I walked away . . .

One day, I walked away.
Didn't say good-bye or see you later.
I just left;
turned my back on the abuse,
leaving your vicious words
in mid air,
in dead silence.
I left the violence,
I left the pain,
I left the "comfort" of my home
to be whole again.

I walked away from the love that was so difficult to hold on to
and so difficult to let go.
(Or maybe, it was no longer there at all).

I walked away from the meaness, the madness, and my sadness.
I walked away from the sorrow so that I could see tomorrow.
I walked away for my children and myself.
I walked away from Death,
and I never looked back,
but,
I walked away.

Celebrating You

You made it,
You came out,
You survived,
You can shout!
You can live,
You can give!

You can move and breathe and have your being!
You have a new way of seeing
yourself,
whole and strong,
tried and true,
you are beautiful too.
You can think, and grow, and love,
you are more than you ever dreamed of
becoming.
You are
a star,
you are
a light,
you have faced
the darkest night,
but hope and courage
carried you
when you did not see your way through.
Through the tunnel to the light,
you are going to be alright!

This poem was formally dedicated to my friend, Janet Billups, a true optimist, who despite her battle with cancer, greeted everybody with the same warm contagious smile. This poem is for her and for every woman who has battled and is battling cancer. It is for every woman who has suffered from domestic violence, lost, tragedy, and any adversity. May you always triumph and may your spirit leap over every obstacle in your path.

Here's to celebrating you, celebrating life.

Storylines

Everyone has a story. All of our stories are meaningful and worthy of being told. There are rags to riches stories, riches to rags stories, happy stories, tragic stories with happy endings and stories that tell of our beginnings. Stories like a kaleidoscope are a combination of many things: histories, experiences, family, education, culture, etc. that make us who we are. There are stories told that give us direction, guidance and hope, and stories that make us contemplate life and help us understand ourselves and others better. There are stories that make us laugh and cry; stories of truth and courage that inspire us about people who have triumphed over adversity and people who have been transformed and reborn. Take the time to listen to somebody's story and share your own story. Every story needs to be heard.

Tell Your Story

Tell your story,
it needs to be heard
by someone who may need
a laugh or a word
to help them believe,
to help them strive,
to teach perseverance,
how you survived.
Tell your story
of your journey through life,
it may reunite
a husband and wife;
it may encourage
lift up and astound
someone who's lost
or someone who's down.
Tell your story,
your "once upon a time,"
the good, the bad,
the rain, the sunshine.
Tell the story
that defines who you are,
what you have done
in your life thus far.
Tell your story
of gains and losses,
victories and defeats,
crowns and crosses.
Tell your story of war and peace;
what battles you've fought
what made them cease;
the troubles, the trials,
the triumphs and success;
tell your story,
for you can tell it best.
Tell your story
of lessons learned
of the medals on your chest,
the scars that you earned.
Tell your story,
your childhood memories
of friends and loved ones
shared with family.

Tell your story
who knows whom it may help
to overcome obstacles
to avoid a misstep.
Your story may guide
or lead someone on;
someone may take hope
from hearing your song.
There are so many stories
that need to be heard
by someone who may need
an encouraging word.
Tell your story,
it may raise a nation,
inspire a king,
make a girl believe
she can accomplish her dream.

Tell your story.

Somebody's Story

My dad left me
when I was three.
He didn't even say good-bye.
My sister
was four
when he walked out the door.
My mother just sat and cried.

She worked two jobs
night and day,
just to make ends meet,
to make sure that we had shelter and clothes
a little food to eat.

Today I stand a grown young man
with my own family,
I cannot do to my children
what my daddy did to me.

I will be a father
I will be a dad
I will give them the life
I never had.
'Go' to their games,
tuck them into bed
and sit with them
while their story's read.
I will take the time
to listen when they talk,
I will be there
when they learn to walk.
I will be their dad
for all their life
to guide and encourage them
through conflict or strife.
I will be there to provide
the things that they need
I will do more than just
'father' a seed.
I will be a nurturer
I will watch them grow
I will be there
and they will know

*what it means to be wanted,
what it means to be loved,
I will be the dad
I always dreamed of.*

*I will be their dad
with joy and with pride
welcoming them home, my arms open wide.*

*I will be their dad
when they fall down,
I will be their dad,
I will never let them down.
I will raise them up; help them on their way,
I will be there for my children, everyday.*

*My dad left me
when I was three;*

He came back today!

*Despite what he did to us,
I welcomed him anyway.
My mother never taught me to hate
she taught me how to go on!
She told me that it's never too late
to rectify a wrong.
Now my children have their grandfather;
my children always have me
and all they even care about
is that we are a family.*

This poem is dedicated to every loving foster parent, grandparent, adoptive parent, aunts, uncles, guardians and others who took care of babies that could not be raised by their birth parents for whatever reason. Some parents give up their children by choice to give them a better life, or until they can get their lives back on track, which though difficult, is unselfish. Others are separated from their parents due to abuse, drugs, hardships, adversities, incarceration, ignorance or abandonment. Nevertheless, many babies grow up to be successful, healthy and happy simply because they were loved and cared for by somebody. This poem is for you.

Somebody took care of that baby

*Somebody took care of that baby
that little bundle of joy
somebody took care of that abandoned girl,
that rejected little boy.
Somebody bathed, clothed and fed
that angel sent to earth,
somebody gave life to that little one
and rejoiced in her birth.
Somebody attended to his needs
and hearken to the cry
of that baby left in the sewer
or in the trash to die.
Somebody's heart was open
to accept that 'special needs' child
somebody took him in
from the streets cold and wild.
Somebody took care of that baby,
made that baby all their own
gave him love and care
'Til that little baby was grown.*

*Somebody took care of that little baby
born addicted to drugs,
held her through her withdrawals,
nurtured her with hugs.*

*Whether by choice or adversity
this life came to be —
I'm glad that somebody took care of that baby,
for that little baby was ME.*

Tug-of-War
(For Linda and Dawn)

They told me that my daughter
has leukemia;
white cells
proliferating,
platelets disintegrating,
creating turmoil
in her bones,
trying to own her body;
traitors!
Can't own her soul;
She is 'mine,'
a gift from God
and life itself.
I birthed this precious child
our blood flowing together
in one continuous circuit,
cells formed from my cells,
but I can't own her
and neither can leukemia.
Blood against blood;
her flesh becoming the rope of our
tug-of-war,
joined cords
'unsevered,'
held taut by the grasp
of my fierce love.
I know her,
her heart still beats within me and,
I will not give her up,
I will not give her up,
I will not give her up,
without a fight!

To the mother who wanted me

Mother, I don't know where I would be
if you had not chosen me,
to love, and care for, to be your child,
to make me laugh, to make me smile.
Because of you, I have thrived,
because of you, I am alive!
And I am the luckiest child on earth,
because your <u>love</u> gave me birth.

Felony

Felony,
committed as a juvenile
wild child
self-identity
crisis,
peer pressure
following the crowd
living out loud.
Petty crimes
then auto theft
mother bereft
lost myself
identity
for a moment
for a while
as a child
running wild.
Juvenile
delinquent —
Mother taught me
better,
tried to fit in
with my friends,
in the end
got a record
a little time
got on track
didn't go back
ever!
Finished school
got a trade
had it made —
but every job
turned me down
though I turned my life
around;
for my mistakes as a juvenile.
Served my time
paid the fine
got on track
didn't go back,
but society
won't set me free
from my juvenile
felony.
Got on track
didn't go back,
there is something
criminal about that —
Felony.

Relapse

Kept getting high
no matter how hard
I tried
to quit;
my body screamed
for more
from every cell to my core;
did so many things
to get high
while life
was passing me by.
Because of drugs
my whole life fell apart —
so if you never tried
to get high,

DON'T START!

High

He was the life of the party,
sitting there
'high as a kite,'
laughing and joking
about everything,
sometimes talking loud
making bunny ears behind
people's heads,
interjecting comments
and playing games.
His eyes were gleaming,
every tooth in his mouth showing
when he grinned.
He was going to be a new daddy,
and he was high,
so high,
on Life.

The Prize Within

He took his sun
and stole away
discreetly
as not to be seen or heard by anyone.
He was full of chagrin and grief,
with no relief.
He felt himself a failure
a dunce,
a dotard,
of no value to anyone.
And since he felt that way
in his mind
it became his reality.
But what he did not know
and did not realize
was that all he needed was a start,
a chance to shine,
for within him
was something great.
He was throwing away a priceless talent —
Himself.

Figure Skating for the Gold

Ready,
dashing out onto the smooth sleek ice
with gracefulness, daring, confidence —
spinning, twirling, leaping high into the air;
suspended, splendid

awe —
then falling down
to the frozen ground,
but
getting up without
breaking a stride,
continuing to skate
in pursuit of the gold
as though the fall
didn't even matter.

Live

Like

That!

You don't know my story
(inspired by Pastor Ada Bailey)

You don't know my story
you don't know my pain
you don't know my history
you may not know my name.
You don't know how I have suffered
been abused as a child
you don't know where I have been,
how long my weary mile.
You don't know my struggle,
the trials I've had to face
you don't know of my adversity
the tragedy I can't erase.
You don't know the days I cried,
the nights I've sat alone,
you don't know what I had to repress
just to continue on.
You don't know my story
you don't know my pain
the things that I have had to endure
my struggle to stay sane.
You don't know what I've faced daily
just to make ends meet
the challenges in my life
the times I met defeat.
You don't know so don't despise me
or judge me by the clothes that I wear
you don't know my brokenness
or the cross I've had to bear.
So since you don't know, be thoughtful
of others who may seem
downcast, withdrawn, or lonely
lacking self-esteem.
You don't know their story
so please don't criticize
the beggar who lost it all,
the addict who tries and tries.
You don't know their story
and you don't know their pain
so be caring to the stranger
and those you know by name.

They may be the child who was abandoned,
or the girl who was abused,
they may be the broken and beaten,
the rejected and refused.
They may be the victim of violence
born of drugs and disease,
Jesus said, "do good
to even the least of these."

[35]"... for I was hungry and you gave me something to eat, I was thirsty and you gave me something to drink, I was a stranger and you welcomed me, [36]I was naked and you gave me clothing, I was sick and you took care of me, I was in prison and you visited me ... [40]Truly I tell you, just as you did it to one of the least of these who are members of my family, you did it to me" (Matthew 25: 35, 36, 40b NRSV).

Wooden Floors

(Make its life worthy of the tree)

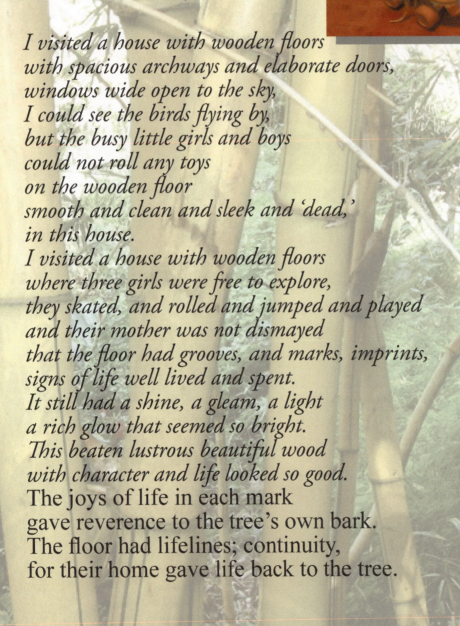

*I visited a house with wooden floors
with spacious archways and elaborate doors,
windows wide open to the sky,
I could see the birds flying by,
but the busy little girls and boys
could not roll any toys
on the wooden floor
smooth and clean and sleek and 'dead,'
in this house.
I visited a house with wooden floors
where three girls were free to explore,
they skated, and rolled and jumped and played
and their mother was not dismayed
that the floor had grooves, and marks, imprints,
signs of life well lived and spent.
It still had a shine, a gleam, a light
a rich glow that seemed so bright.
This beaten lustrous beautiful wood
with character and life looked so good.
The joys of life in each mark
gave reverence to the tree's own bark.
The floor had lifelines; continuity,
for their home gave life back to the tree.*

Growth Spurts

Bodies stretching overnight,
limbs growing,
voices changing,
physiological rearrangements
forcing organs and cells to
expand on command.
Growth spurts
at any age,
pushing us,
expanding us beyond past thoughts and ideas,
transforming us, reshaping us,
making us see where we were once blind,
innocent, and failing to realize that we didn't know that we
didn't know.
We grow
when life demands a change,
when plans fall apart,
when dreams are deferred,
when friends leave,
when time fades,
when health wanes, and
when Death comes knocking.
We grow when we fail,
when we make mistakes and don't
understand
when and where we went wrong.
We wake up and find ourselves in a different place
with different ideas and plans because experiences jolt us
to new realities, possibilities, perplexities and epiphanies
all at once;
foresight beginning to precede hindsight more often,
and our peripheral vision becomes mature as we see
clearer in the mirror that no longer hides our flaws
but forces us to unmask,
reveal,
be real—
then we grow;
an internal metamorphosis.
When we don't grow
don't expand
closing our eyes,
stopping our ears,

resisting change,
stunting our growth,
we become 'dwarfs'
living in fairytales with the same beginnings and the same endings everyday.
Growth spurts take us outside of the enchanted forest and gives us the sky.
Growth spurts, stretching us,
leaving us longing,
un-content to be content.
Growth spurts
sometimes painful,
expand us,
strengthens us,
shakes our minds,
deepens our thoughts,
straightens our backbones,
growing us wings,
and every now and then,
we Fly.

Lifeline

Lord, help me be slow to criticize
for I want to help my brother rise,
let me not be quick to put my sister down
when she is trying to turn her life around,
for in whatever situation they may be
help me remember, it could be me.
So teach me to be humble in my success
not thinking of others as being less,
not knowing the battles they have fought
nor the pain their life has brought,
for I may not know and may not see
how close to breaking they may be.
So let my words be uplifting and kind,
let me be to them a steady lifeline,
for in my dark days and on my stormy sea,
they may be the one
to be a lifeline for me.

Lines

Today I looked into my mind
only to find
line
      upon
           line.
My thoughts are somewhere
behind each line
and I feel like a prisoner
serving time
in my own mind;
yet, I know that
love,
patience, and
understanding from you,
is the key,
to set me free.

Life's beauty marks

Behold the beauty marks in my face,
they are signs of living grace.
Behold the silver hairs that crown my head
and the laugh lines which dance around my twinkling eyes
and my smile;
for they tell the story of joy and pain,
of cloudy days, of sun and rain;
remnants of a blushing bride,
and a baby that was her father's pride.
They still harbor the smile of a child,
and the friend who went an extra mile.
And for all the children that I have seen,
my eyes still hold a special gleam,
from kissing cheeks, and laughing out loud,
teaching, preaching, and walking proud.
These lines show time and
experiences gained,
treasured within this mortal
frame.
There is a story in every line
of this human touched by the
Divine,
who has lived
and loved and lost,
and sometimes had to bear a cross
that weighed upon this furrowed brow
but made me wiser and stronger now.
These lifelines hold special memories
of the gifts and love life brought to me.
And every sunset, and every sunrise
enhances the beauty of my twinkling eyes.

CHILDREN

I have always loved children. They bring joy and laughter to my soul. I love watching them learn new words and new things as they explore their surroundings. They bring an excitement to every new discovery and accomplishment. They bring a newness and richness to life everyday.
Their acceptance of others and freedom to express love is something divine. Children have always given me my most happiest moments, a reason to smile, hope, and live with a greater purpose. I love reminiscing with my adult nieces and nephews about the many funny and interesting things they have done and said as they were growing up.
This section is dedicated to all of my nieces, nephews, cousins and all the children who enrich my life everyday.

CHILDREN

(for Maya, Mikaela, MaKenzie, Dyson, Tylin, Amari, Mikai, Ryan, and all my children)

Children;
eyes open wide
with surprise
and endless curiosity;
faces flushed
feet that rush
or jump,
or skip,
or hop,
non-stop . . .
Little fingers,
little hands,
little minds
to expand,
walking,
talking,
having fun,
learning, growing,
from sun to sun,
capturing our hearts
with cherub smiles
making life's moments
all worthwhile.
Sweetness, innocence,
and delight,
opening up our insights
to joy and life,
and hope and pleasure,
the jewels and gems
of life's great treasure —
Children.

It still takes a village . . .

Encourage a child today,
guide them on their way
to becoming a productive woman or man,
help them grow; help them stand,
give them sound wisdom, good advice,
be a mentor in their life,
work together with common concern,
help them dream; help them learn.
For the world will be a better place
if we would wholeheartedly embrace
all the children of every race.

Be a bridge, be a light,
promote the good; uphold the right.
Show love, mercy and brotherhood;
promote justice for our common good.
Give them a voice; let them have their say,
and even if they go astray,
gently show them a better way.
Uplift them, make them strong,
emphasize their strengths; help them rectify their wrongs.
For the world will be a better place
if we would wholeheartedly embrace
all the children of every race.

Accept them and love them for who they are,
your encouragement will carry them far,
to the highest heights that they can reach
when we practice what we preach.
And should they stumble trying to find their way,
let us not cast them away —
Reach for those who are abused and lost,
restore their hope at any cost,
steady their feet to tread a path,
uplift their hearts that they can laugh.
Unveil their beauty deep within,
help them believe in themselves again.
For the world will be a better place
if we would wholeheartedly embrace
all the children of every race.

48 Lifelines

It still takes a village . . .

Our greatest human achievements are not the physical walls that we tear down, but the people that we build up.

Families: Building Bridges for New Beginnings

Every time a baby is born,
it's a new beginning,
whether it's a girl or boy,
it's a new beginning —
watching them walk and talk and grow,
releasing them and letting them go
to *start* their *beginning* . . .
But beginnings and beginnings are what make families grow,
and it is love that connects us, from the seeds that we sow.
This one 'begets' this one, and that one 'begets' another;
boys become dads; girls become mothers, with soul mates producing,
the *sisters* and *brothers,*
who become *aunts* and *uncles* to *nephews* and *nieces*
while *in-laws* join, and the family increases.
Cousins, first, second, third, and on and on and on,
forming the bridges that we rely upon.
Parents become *grandparents* imparting wisdom to us all,
steadying our foundation, helping us walk tall.
Families are here to remind us
that we have a history,
a beginning of who we are, and how we came to be.
They are there to journey with us, as we live and grow,
celebrating life together, through the years that come and go.
They are there to stand with us,
to guide, support, to feel,
reminding us everyday,
that life is precious and real.
And life is always beginning, for new beginnings are everyday,
as we daily teach our children, to help them on their way.
New beginnings are now, and the bridges that we build
will guide our children, to a life that is fulfilled;
to success in their endeavors, to a love which knows no end,
and family is where it all begins.
Rooted and grounded and interconnected,
the circle of life being perfected . . .

I Want a Forever Love

I want a forever love,

a love not dampened by time or trials we face,

I want a love that forgives, and knows the meaning of grace.

I want a love that is real and strong

yet gentle enough to amend any wrong.

I want a love that blossoms with each season

and needs no greater reason to celebrate

other than for the sake of loving and being loved.

I want a forever love with you.

Seeking Hearts

Lord, I desire a woman who loves you so much that with her first waking breath, you are praised.
I desire a woman whose home and walls echo your name reverberating your praise
all her days,
a virtuous woman created in your image
who pursues the heart of the one who created her, and the one from which she was made;
A woman that I can love and cherish as a wife, all my life.

I will follow a woman who is humble enough to follow you.
I will love a woman who loves you.
I will live forever with a woman who will live her life unto you.

Lord, I desire a man who loves you so much that with his first waking breath, you are praised.
A man whose house and walls echo your name reverberating your praise all his days,
a man created in your image
who is not ashamed to pursue the heart of the one who created him;
knowing that you are his strength
in everything!

I will follow a man who is humble enough to follow you,
who will lead his house in serving you too.
I will love a man whose ways are true
a man whose life will honor you.

Love is Magical

Love is magical, but it does not disappear.
It is like a fantasy, but it does not dissolve with the next thought—
Love is tangible,
    visible, and permanent,
      a dream come true,
because love is me and you.

Love Grows

Love
  grows,
    love shows,

water it,
nurture it,
prune it,
cherish it,
and you will keep it
    ALIVE
      Forever.

"Love never fails" I Cor 13:8 (NIV)

Promise

Today is the day of many days to come
as we stand together in this moment as one,
with our hopes and hearts full of life
as we become husband and wife,

To live and love as God commands
to support one another so that together we can stand
through the triumphs and trials that we may face
and learn the meaning of giving grace.

Throughout our lives, the sun and the rain
we will trust our love to sustain
our hearts and hopes that they will remain true,
and everyday, I promise, I will love you.

Living Faith

FAITH
*It looks beyond my inadequacies
to the realm of my possibilities,
it draws on my capabilities,
making my hopes,* **realities.**

Answering Moses

Moses said, "Show me your glory..."
(Exodus 33:18 NRSV)

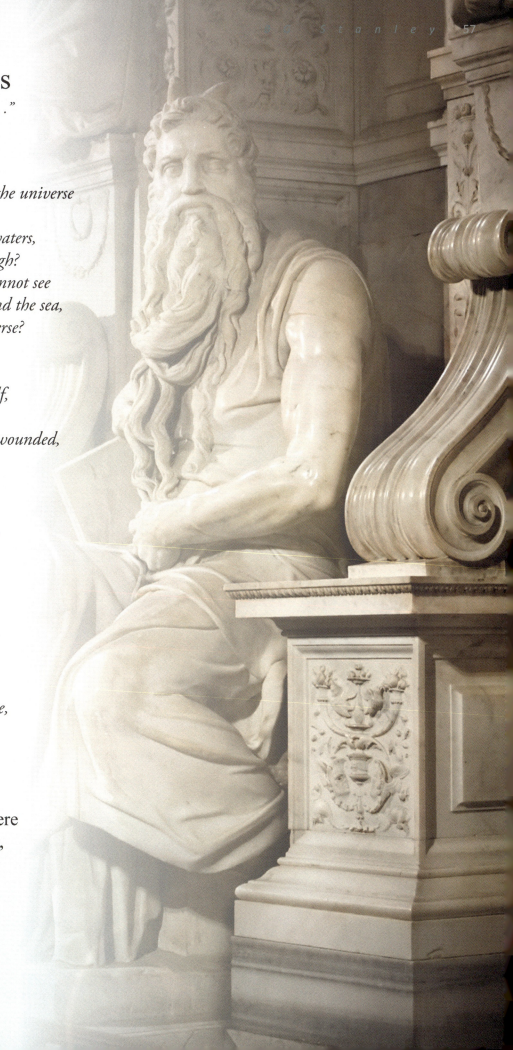

Where is this God who rules the universe
and who commands the sky;
the one who rolled back the waters,
sent down manna from on high?
Where is this 'being' who I cannot see
who commanded the wind and the sea,
where is this God of the universe?
Show yourself to me.

Awake, arise, and show thyself,
stop these wars that maim,
stretch your hand to save the wounded,
Jehovah is your name.
Can you not prevent
the chaos in the universe,
earthquakes that destroy lives,
babies malformed at birth?
What is your answer,
to the hungry child that cries,
how can they see you God,
when bombs light their skies?
Where are you God,
in the deep dark abyss;
Tragedies, sickness, and disease,
are you present in all this?

Human hands create wars,
injustice and oppression,
violence, terrorism, anywhere
from apathy and regression,

but,

*through human hands and human hearts
God works everyday,
binding up the broken,
helping the lost find their way.
God has never stopped caring
for the people on this Earth,
for God is revealed in human flesh
and missions that give birth
to compassionate hearts that answer
the question of all time,
"Yes, I am my brother's keeper,
and my brother he is mine."*

*In the kindness of a 'stranger'
 familiarity,
it is the presence of God
dwelling in humanity.
And though sometimes we wrestle
with questions that bring us doubt
God works through humanity
to help bring us out.*

*See God there in Haiti
with the victims of the quake,
while you are slumbering
God is still awake
soothing broken women
raped and scorned
caring for sick babies
to addicted mothers born.
Down in the Motherland
where AIDS is taking lives,
God is caring for orphans
helping them survive.
Even in the prison
God visits us,
transforming the penitent,
forgiving the unjust.*

*God is on the battlefield,
cradling dying men,
helping negotiate solutions
as we pray for wars to end.
Talking in the streets against violence,
voices raised in protest,
for God is never silent
where there is social unrest,
neither blind to injustice,
nor deaf to the cry of the weak,
people looking for comfort,
from you the answers they seek.
Answering the call
of someone in despair,
look Moses see and hear,
God everywhere.
Everywhere there is love,
even where there is pain,
God is there to answer
calling someone's name.
"Go," is the command God gives,
"Go," and do my will,
and those who serve with compassion
show that God is real.*

"I had heard you with my ears, but now I see you with my eyes. . ." Job 42:5 (Tanakh)

" The just shall live by faith"

Recession —
and we survive
for one more day.
Yesterday was not easy;
not enough money
for bills
and food —
no jobs, anywhere;
losing my neighbors
because of foreclosures.
Creditors calling
every minute
demanding water
from a rock,
but I am standing
on a rock,
Christ —
which is
the only reason
I'm even standing
at all.

*Though the fig tree does not blossom,
and no fruit is on the vine; yet I will
rejoice in the Lord; I will exult in the
God of my salvation.
(Habakkuk 3: 17-18 NRSV)*

I Am

I am faith that reaches and touches the heart of Christ through the hem of his garment.
I am faith that causes the cripple man to convince his friends to lower him through the roof so that Jesus could heal him.
I am faith that reaches, teaches, and preaches
regarding not the obstacles or mountains that seem so large
but crumble at the words of Christ:
"Be moved, be healed, be free, and be whole."
I am faith, and I am bold.
I am faith because
I am. . .
I don't even need to walk on water
because the water is in me
coursing through my veins
like a river
springing up into life,
never dry,
overflowing, and
growing
because, the "I Am who I am"
is all that I need
in me.
I AM Faith.

Faith in the Desert

I thank God for the desert
for every oasis I've seen
appeared when I had nothing left to do but dream.
In the dryness of the desert
where no water 'is'
I found my thirst quenched
by my own penitent tears.
It was in the dryness of the desert
with the sun beating on my head
that I found a sacred place
to make a soothing bed.
In the cradle of the rock
the Lord let me hide
and when I could go no further
God walked right by my side.
I could lean upon God's shoulder
when my eyes were too tired to see.
When my back was too weary to carry my load
my God did not forsake me.
In the dryness of the desert
the vultures awaited my death
delirious with thirst and hunger,
I had nothing left.
No will to live, anguish and pain
my bones like dust, bereft,
but God sustained me with his love,
and restored my failing health.
So I walked on through the desert
and I walked in perfect peace
for in the dryness of the desert,
my faith and hope increased.
In the dryness of the desert
I found water for my thirst
when I communed with the bread of life
and learned to put God first.
So I thank God for the desert
for my famine and my feast,
for in the dryness of the desert,
my faith and hope increased.

Worship begins within

If my life is not a praise of you Lord,
then how can I give you praise?
If I offer not myself as a living sacrifice,
then how can I bring an offering?
If I do not give from my heart,
then how can I give my gift?
If I do not love those whom I have seen,
then how can I love you Lord?
If my body is not a temple for the Holy Spirit to dwell in,
then how, and where, can I worship?

I will be an instrument for thee

Lord, you are the beating of my heart,
the marrow in my bones,
the blood that courses through my veins.
You are the breath in my lungs,
and I will be an instrument for thee.

Untitled

I went higher in God
when I humbled myself (Luke 18: 14).
I became wiser
when I became a fool for Christ (I Corinthians 1: 25).
I was fulfilled
when I became empty of 'self, '
and I found contentment (Phil 4:11, I Timothy 6:6).

I became poor in spirit
and inherited the kingdom of heaven (Matthew 5:4).
I laid down all my earthly goods,
and God made me rich (II Corinthians 6:10).
Everyday I die, (I Corinthians 15:31)
but Christ makes me alive! (Galatians 2:20)

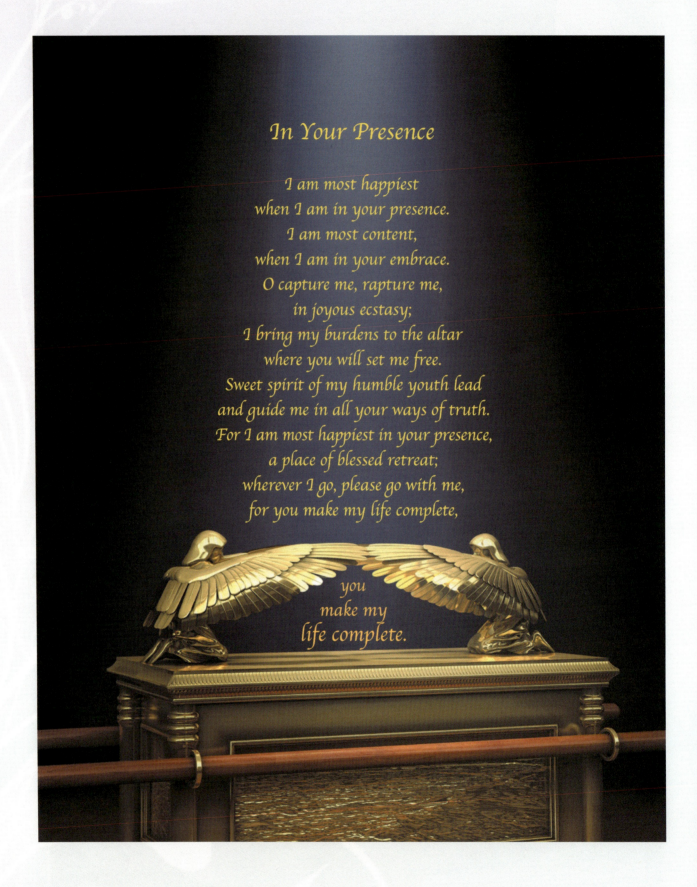

In Your Presence

I am most happiest
when I am in your presence.
I am most content,
when I am in your embrace.
O capture me, rapture me,
in joyous ecstasy;
I bring my burdens to the altar
where you will set me free.
Sweet spirit of my humble youth lead
and guide me in all your ways of truth.
For I am most happiest in your presence,
a place of blessed retreat;
wherever I go, please go with me,
for you make my life complete,

you
make my
life complete.

Reflection

Lord,
let me live for you
live like you
live unto you
as you live, in me.
Teach me to love as you loved,
when loved, you loved,

when unloved, you still loved —
no difference.
Teach me to be as kind to others
as you have been to me,
that they will see 'you'
when they see me.

Hope

Would I have my dreams unfilled
and sink like a reckless lost ship
where roaring waters my boat fill
and make me lose my grip,
where storms hover over my silent head
tearing my sail to the ground
while I helplessly struggle though half dead
so that my banner won't go down?
Though all my life slants like a slope
with the rugged tempest and rains
I know for certain my eternal hope
will revive me once again.
Though all things seem to fade away,
The light of hope will guide my way.

"Now faith is being sure of what we hope for and certain of what we do not see." Hebrews 11:1 (NIV Bible)

Survival

A volcano erupted and smothered me with the heat of *hell*.
I rose, only to be tossed into a *raging sea*,
and down into an *endless pit*.
Life was a struggle, and I could not survive.

I was bound in hell by hate,
malice, strife, and despair were my constant foes,
night and day on turbulent waters I sank,
nearly drowned by futile attempts to survive heartache and grief,
I lay down to die.

I lost everything, but found nothing.
Each blow I received scarred me.
I was burned with charcoals of misfortune,
lashed with confusion by winds upon dashing seas
and drowned by darkness in an endless pit of troubles.

I ran for my life as I begged for unseen mercy.
Where was my hope?
Where was my joy?
Where was my peace?
Where was my comfort?
Where was my love?
Swallowed up in misery?

When all my bones were broken and my spirits deterred
I bowed down to Death.
I wanted it all to end,
I no longer cared.
Please take my life, but God said, "Go on."

So I was forced to endure and tolerate life in hell
until I became strong and bold.
I lived in the waters, until I learned to swim.
I lived in the pit, until I learned to climb.
I lived, until I learned to survive.

And I became a rock and a survivor
with an unbreakable soul
and an indestructible mind.

I had learned to blossom like a flower amid thorns —
I was alive!

For one beautiful day, the 'Sun' touched me
and I rose over all the obstacles
and mountains in my way
and became a bridge for others over my former troubled waters.

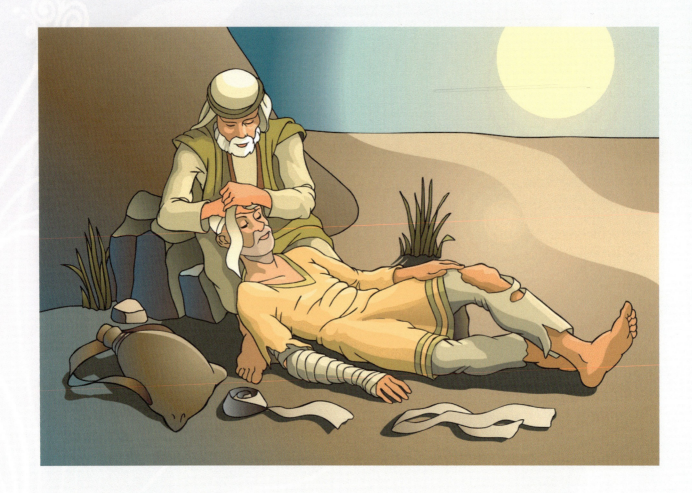

Samaritans

On every Jericho road I've been
God has sent along a Samaritan.
When others scoffed and passed me by,
God sent a Samaritan, so that I would not die;
to bind my wounds, to heal my heart,
to show me love, some joy impart.
Now every time I walk down a Jericho road,
and a wounded soul I see,
I become a Samaritan,
because someone was a Samaritan for me.

The best gift

Nothing,
that's what you got,
nothing,
if you don't have love.
You may prophesy, testify, and amplify,
but it doesn't glorify
God,
if you don't have love.
You may give your body to the flames
all your wealth and knowledge vain,
all your eloquence sounding brass,
noisy cymbals that will not last,
if you don't have love.
Love gives kindness,
love shows care,
not just to some,
but to people everywhere.
It trusts and protects, "love never fails,"
it hopes, perseveres, 'til all is well.
Love increases; becomes *mature,*
always guided by motives pure.
It is patient and understanding,
not easily disturbed
because love lives and walks
according to God's word.
Love thinks no evil, seeks no revenge,
rejoices not in wrong, or records 'past' sins.
Not envious, rude, arrogant or proud,
neither is love boastfully loud.
But nothing
is what you got
if you don't have love.
You can have faith to move mountains,
no doubt —
you can sing like an angel,
you can preach and shout,
but without love,
it is nothing,
'cause love is what its all about.

(I Corinthians 13 chapter, NIV)

Signs of Life

Giving Life

I thought about the cycle of life and reproduction. Animals, plants and humans reproduce life. I once heard a man say, "That is all that we are here for, to reproduce." I initially thought, "that's all?" Yet, what greater thing than reproducing life; that in and of itself is a miraculous gift, but producing life is much more than a physiological process. There are people who do not physically reproduce children, but they give life, for giving life means, giving life meaning. Some may reproduce a life but abandon or abuse that life taking away its meaning, robbing that life of its purpose. Some reproduce life and unselfishly give that life up for adoption. People who adopt or rescue children and animals caring for them and nurturing them save their lives because they give them life. They give them life because they, like loving parents, give them meaning and validation through which they can develop and achieve their own purpose.

People who lift people up give life.

People who donate organs, blood and bone marrow; give life. Those who sponsor the hungry and homeless, give life. People who care for and take time with our silver citizens, give life. People who volunteer or work with children and children with special needs, give life. Those who help change the life of a troubled teen or shelter the abused from domestic violence, give life. The tireless workers and volunteers who rush to rescue victims of disaster, give life. Those who sponsor a child's college education or teach someone to read, give life. People who actively stand by the recovering alcoholic or drug addict, give life. People who fight for social justice and the rights of others, give life, for freedom and independence is liberating. Therefore, even if we do not or cannot physically reproduce another human being, we can give life in so many ways.

Giving life is like giving nourishment to a plant or flower.

If a dying plant or flower is given the essential elements of sun, soil and water along with love and care, it springs forth beyond its own limitations of growth because that life gives life to new life — forever. It is the care and the love that we give to others that cause them to spring forth and even grow beyond their limitations. It enables and motivates them by bringing life within their being so that they can then fulfill their own purpose or goals. Giving life, gives us life. All of us who have life have the potential to give life. Many who have been given life, like an endless vine, expand that gift to others and are enriched beyond words. Giving and receiving life transcends physiological existence. *Giving life makes life more meaningful and unending.*

Keep giving,

Keep living!

When somebody loves you

When somebody loves you
you can see it in their eyes
and in the loving glances they make
even when you are not looking.
When somebody loves you
you can see it in their smile
and in the way they light up in your presence
or at the mention of your name.
When somebody loves you
the mere thought of them
can lift you up
on a rough day.
When somebody loves you
You can feel it in their touch
and in the thoughtful things that they do.
When somebody loves you
you can hear it in their voice,
and even when they say nothing at all
you can hear it so loudly,

What's Important to You?

What's important to you
in your daily life,
the hustle and bustle
of deadlines to meet
work to complete,
money to make
bills to pay,
what's on your calendar
to accomplish today?
What's on your schedule,
how much time
to finish the things
you had in mind?
Giving your all, and giving your best
do you take any time
to just sit and rest?

Take a breath . . .

What's important to you
in the hours of your life,
spending time with your wife,
becoming the richest in the world,
or laughing and playing
with your boys and girls;
which is more fulfilling
than anything
that life can offer

or money can bring?
What's important to you,
what gets you out of bed,
what drives and motivates you
besides getting ahead?

What's important to you,
the vase that fell,
or the comfort in knowing
that your children are well?
Does your house always need to be
as 'neat as a pin,' or can it just be
a home to live in?
Yes, things are special, but are you overly obsessed
with luxuries that are meaningless
that you cannot take time
to sit with a friend
or dance to no end?
What's important to you,
status and fame,
wanting the world to know your name,
or feeding the hungry,
the sick and the lame
wherein lies true glory
untainted by fame?
Salute a soldier
who has fought hard and long
for your rights and freedoms;
to live, to belong.
Cut a log for the old man
who lives down the street
so that in the cold winter
he can have heat.
There are so many things
in life we can do
but you must take time
for what's important too.
What's important to you
in your life every day
how do you spend your time
or give love away?
Pause and contemplate
what is real, what is true,
meaningful, lasting, and important to you.

Go back to school; get a degree,
take a trade,
or just live free
from the bondage of fear and not venturing out,
inhale nature's beauty

*stand and shout.
Travel the world,
fish if you like,
go camping, canoeing,
or take a long hike.
What's important to you
to fulfill your dreams
to accomplish your goals
whether young or old;
for age has no bearing
on one's success
live and do
what you love best.
Do what is needed,
what matters most
raise your glass
to what you would toast.
Let the phone ring
and conversate
with your teens and loved ones
or make a date
with your parents who've been there
for you all your life;
say a prayer to end wars
suffering and strife.*

*Take time
not just for things
or objects and such
take time for the people
who love you so much.*

*Take a moment for faith
to worship as you please
meditate within,
or bow on your knees.*

*What's important to you
from life's offerings?
what makes you smile
what makes your heart sing?*

*Marvel at all the things that you can see and do
that make life so meaningful
and important to you.*

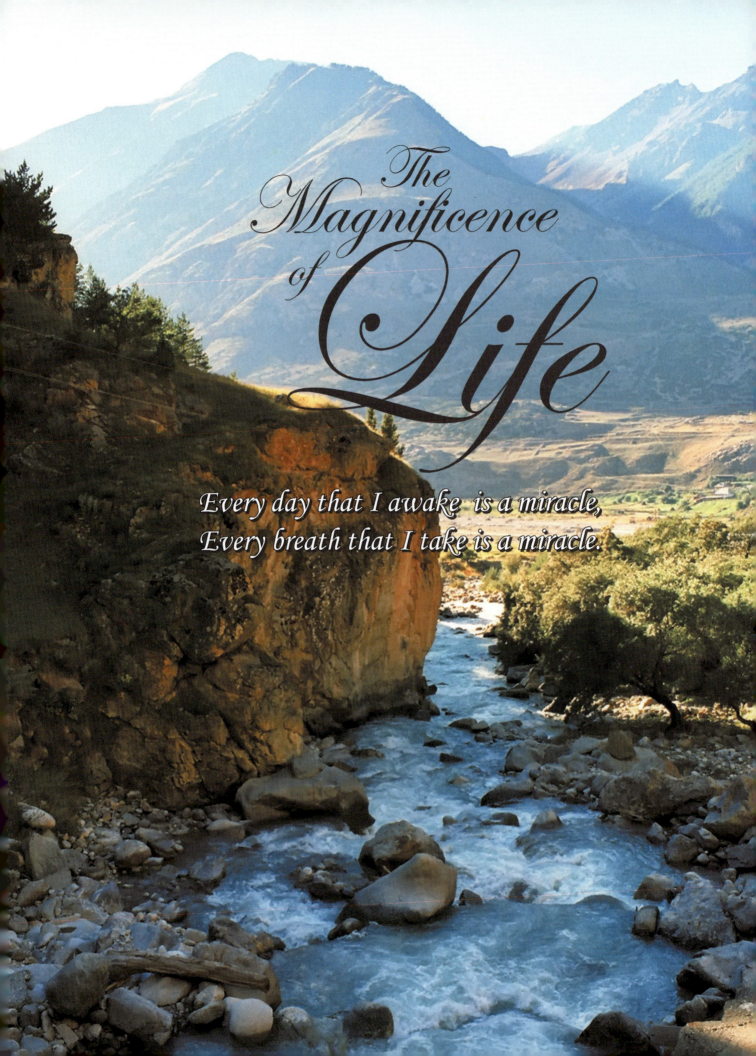

"Our Lives can change with every breath we take"

In the movie, "Where the Heart Is," produced by Susan Cartsonis, actress Natalie Portman comforted her friend with these words, "Our lives can change with every breath we take." The truth about this statement is that it is so real; our lives can change from moment to moment, from breath to breath in so many ways, some within our control and some beyond our control. Some changes are good, and some are not. Some we can foresee, and some we cannot, like heart attacks, strokes, aneurysms, accidents, weather disasters and so on. Things like these are so earth shattering, so devastating that if we had no faith or a belief in God we would simply crumble.

God sits with us on our mourner's bench and walks with us in our lowest valley. I believe that God is in the people who are there with us during the greatest crises of our lives when no words can comfort, and nothing makes sense. What does make sense is life; living, breathing, moving, talking, laughing, singing, eating; just being, it all flows so naturally, so routinely, we hardly notice the magnificence of it all. The magnificence of a brain that deciphers and interprets tons of information in the 'blink of an eye' is phenomenal. Eyes that see far, near and around at the same time, and ears that hear through sound waves that vibrate against a drum to be interpreted by a brain where synapses occur in milliseconds is beyond amazing.

The beating heart, the inhaling and exhaling lungs exchanging gases with nature is overwhelmingly profound, and powerfully magnificent.

Life occurs in many moments, many days, many months, many weeks, many years, and many breaths. Contemplate the magnificence of life to help assuage the sadness of death and tragedies that occur in one moment; for only one breath separates life and death. Death is once, but life is everyday. So every day that you live; laugh, love, and cry, with those whom you hold dear, and praise God for being present in this world today. Take not one living thing or person for granted. Inhale the magnificence of each moment and the magnificence of life in everything: humans, animals, and nature. Contemplate your very existence and being in this moment for "our lives can change with every breath we take."

Let me live Lord with an understanding and appreciation of the magnificence of Life.

The Magnificence of Life

Great wonders and marvels the Earth does hold,
everyday new mysteries unfold
as fascinating histories are retold
from dinosaur bones to California gold—
But the greatest wonder of the world
is the miraculous birth of every boy and girl.
And words alone could not define
the masterpieces of the Divine.
From the Rocky Mountains to the Niagara Falls
God spoke the word and made them all,
from the brightest star in the darkest sky
the planets and galaxies floating by,
rushing waters, dashing waves,
trees and grasses, paths unpaved,
animals, reptiles, birds of every kind
bear the imprint of something divine.
The living, moving, breathing beings
more magnificent than anything;
hearts that beat and legs that walk,
how we hear, see, and talk,
are scientifically well defined by brilliant and creative minds.
And I believe without a doubt
we really have little to debate about
for both science and God helps us understand,
The magnificence of life,
The magnificence of man/woman.

Bless this sanctuary called Earth

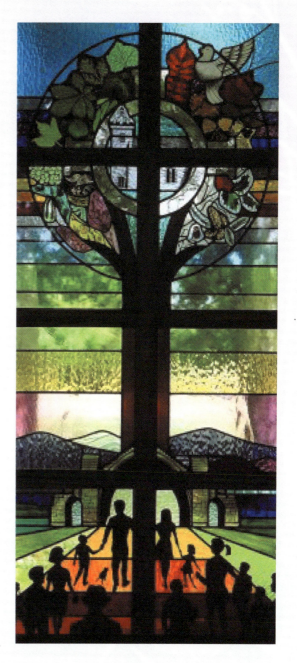

Bless this sanctuary called Earth,
bless this place oh God,
bless this sanctuary called Earth,
where many lives have trod.
Bless this sanctuary called Earth
replenish it with new birth,
new trees and seas
new birds and bees
new babes and beast
let the earth increase;
new life in every place
as trees bow to worship your face,
and birds high in the sky
sing praises as they fly by,
while young and old gather
full of joy and mirth
praising God for the 'magnificence of life'
in this sanctuary called Earth.

Praise the Lord from the Earth, Praise God in his sanctuary;
Let everything that breathes praise the Lord.
(Psalms 148:7a; Psalms 150: verses 1a, 6, NRSV)

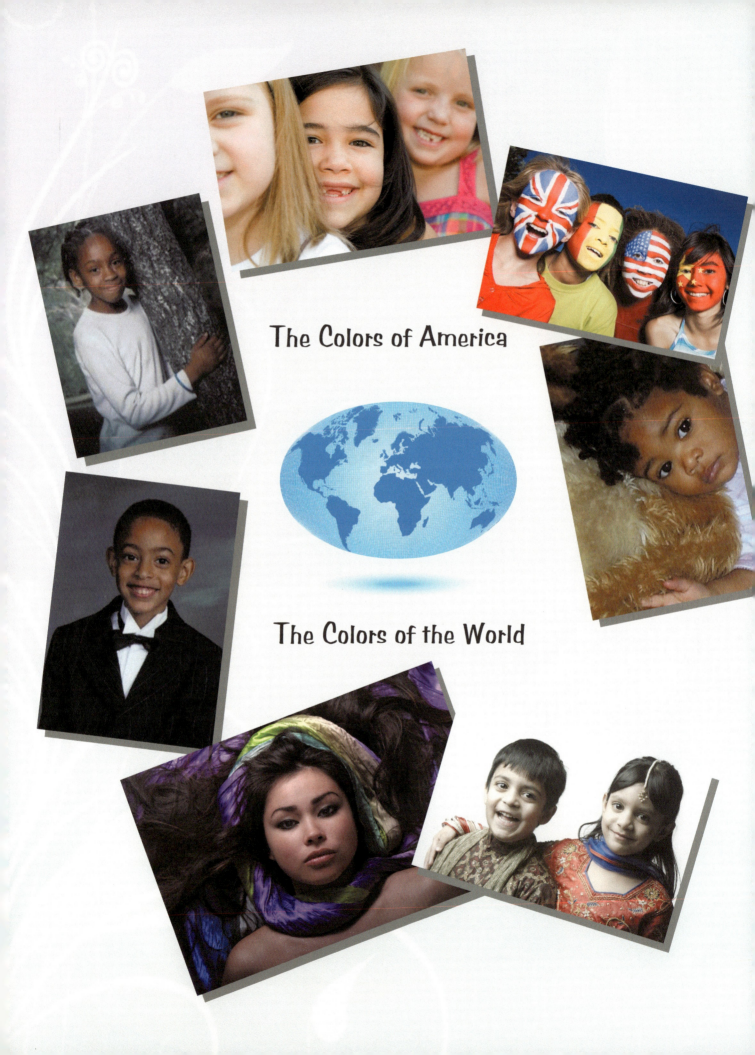

The 'Colors of America' was designed for children. Its purpose is to encourage the children to celebrate their origins and the rich diversity found here in America and in the world. It is through learning histories, cultures, interaction and dialogue that we develop tolerance and acceptance of others without prejudices.

There are groups that continue to promote segregation, discrimination, intolerance, bullying and inequality; therefore, we must raise a generation of children who will counter the negative stereotyping through knowledge and relationships.

I want the children to enlighten their parents and the world about our differences and similarities and teach others how to celebrate those unique and special differences. When we share our cultures and become acquainted with people of different genders, ethnicities, cultures, and languages, we are enriched and enlightened in so many ways.

I encourage the children to teach and show all of us that the beauty of America lies in the freedoms and diversity of America, for the true colors of America are red, white and blue, with '**stars of every hue**.'

BG Stanley (brim4peace)

The Colors of America

In the red, white, and blue
there are people of every hue,
pledging allegiance,
pledging to be true,
to the ideas of freedom
justice and liberty,
so many colors,
such rich *diversity*.
So many histories,
so many ideas,
so many stories,
lives that are real,
of people who struggled
and for freedom died
in America the beautiful
where I freely reside.
So many ethnicities,
peoples from every shore
coming to America
through her welcome door,
becoming citizens of this nation
pledging to be true,
pledging dedication,
to the red, white, and blue.

So many faces...

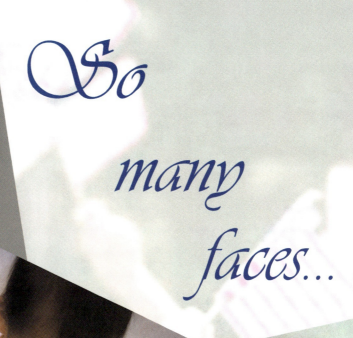

So many smiles...

Ignorance
does not see or hear.
It thinks negatively of others
without learning,
without knowing.
It cannot grow,
but it can be passed down
from generation to generation —
a deliberate curse.
Ignorance,
is embedded with fear,
distrust,
conjuring threats
and
conspiracies,
out of nothing.
It believes in false ideas and irrational theories.
It is an impedance to unity
and diplomacy because ignorance creates wars
where peace abounds.
It thinks that others are not
competent and capable, though they are,
because it believes in hierarchies of gender and race
and that there are *superior* and *inferior* human beings in this world.
It cannot appreciate the beauty and diversity of colors and cultures.
It misses out on so much knowledge and friendships
because it applies negative stereotypes and generalizations to those who are different
making judgments of others at first sight
without knowing the content of their character.
Ignorance does not attempt
to learn, or reach out of its own dark mind.
It chooses to remain socially 'dumb'
and 'deaf'
and 'blind'
to the greatness of the diversity of humankind.
Ignorance,
rise
above
it!

The King's Dream

The King's Dream

(Dedicated to all of my friends who have enriched my life because of the content of their character).

The rods and cones in our eyes
see black and white and color,
the faces and shapes our eyes outline
are then interpreted by our mind
that defines
what we see, think and feel,
imagined, interpreted or even real.
So we are not colorblind,
but blinded by our own mind
when we see colors in a negative light
judging wrongly at first sight.

This is what the dreamer encouraged the world to see —
the essence of all humanity
tied up in a garment of destiny
that inextricably connects you to me[1],
and the content of our character within
holds more meaning than the color of our skin.

> So SEE ME; get to know ME,
> my character and my name,
> you may enrich my life,
> for yours I'll do the same.
> SEE ME; get to know me,
> my character and my name,
> for beneath all of our beautiful colors
> we are all so much the same.

---

[1] Dr. Martin Luther King, Jr.

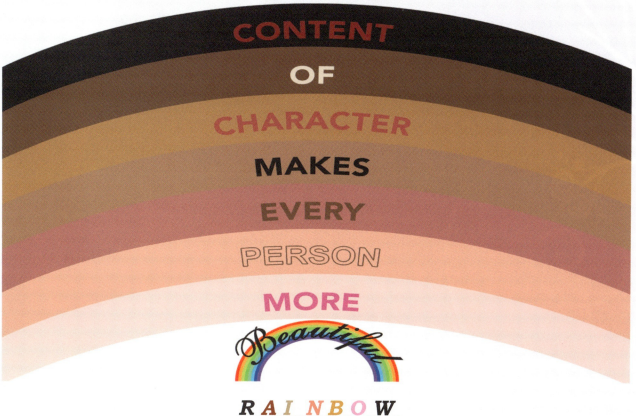

The most magnificent rainbow I have seen
is the rainbow of King's dream,
formed from the many shades and colors of skin,
enhanced by a content of character within;
that includes respectfulness, trustworthiness and care,
good citizenship, responsibility, being just and fair
to all the colors of this connective blend
that makes us brothers, sisters, and friends —
unclouded by racism, hatred and lies,
this is the rainbow that brightens our skies.
This is the rainbow that rose from the storm
to promote equality and justice
from which we were born.
This is the rainbow that leads to the gold,
this is the rainbow of beautiful souls.

We are all People
(Written for Camp Diversity.)

We are all people,
We are human beings,
in many ways we are different,
but we share many things.
We may be different weights and heights,
skin color, gender and hair,
but we are all people,
humanity we share.
We all listen to music,
we eat foods we like,
we wear clothes and wash our hair,
we sometimes ride our bikes.

We dance, we sing, we laugh, we cry,
we love, we live, we're born, we die,
'cause we are all people,
we are human beings,
we may be different in many ways
but we share so many things.
We are from many cultures,
from here and lands afar
so let's celebrate our diversity,
and celebrate who we are.
For it does not matter
where we are from
or how we say our names,
we are *different* and *alike* in many ways,
but we are people, *'just'* the same.

Because of You

This section is dedicated to the legendary Civil Rights Activists in America, the Women Suffragists, and to Human Rights Activists everywhere.

A Letter of Thanks

To all my heroes and sheroes of the Civil Rights Movement in America let me express my deepest gratitude for the sacrifices and commitments you made in order to obtain civil liberties and justice for America's Black citizens. I am so sorry for the suffering and humiliation that you had to endure in order to obtain equal rights and opportunities for many who may have otherwise been denied. I thank the young students who walked into schools where they were not wanted despite the ridicule and threats. I also thank the students who sat at lunch counters where they were not served, and those who risked their lives on buses for freedom. I am also applauding the White men and women who refused to follow the status quo or become complacent and ambivalent to the inequities and injustices inflicted on America's Black citizens. What a difference you all have made in this world. You are all outstanding human beings. It is because of you that many of us have reached our goals and fulfilled our dreams, and many will continue to pursue their goals and fulfill their dreams. There are those who say that we must forget that history, but how can we forget that sacred history that has taught all of us valuable lessons of humanity?

How can we ever forget you? Every time I sit in a restaurant, attend a university of my choice, or sit wherever I want to on a bus or train, I think of you. Every time I go and vote for the candidate of my choice, I think of you with honor and pride. Your tenacity and "soul force" was not only instrumental in improving the lives of Black American citizens, but for every American, and for all who would come to America from the nations of the world. You disseminated the work of transformation. You raised the level of consciousness and humanity. We are all elevated by your unyielding efforts. Nevertheless, we know that there are still disparities, inequities and injustices that we must continue to redress, but you gave us a foundation and a starting point along with the hope and courage to continue to make changes. So please, accept this letter as an expression of the magnitude of my gratitude for all that you have done.

Because of you, many Blacks and Whites are friends, neighbors, and partners and their lives are forever enriched. Many meaningful relationships exist between races today because of you. You turned indignity into honor, violence into non-violence and segregation into integration with an appreciation and acceptance of diversity. You have opened so many closed doors of opportunity in education, politics, sports, philanthropy, technology and the arts and sciences. Because of you, many have made, and are still making significant contributions to America and the world. Because of you, I, and so many others can and do thrive in America. Because of you... because of all of you. May God forever bless the works of your hands. You have my deepest thanks and highest respect.

BG Stanley

Because of You

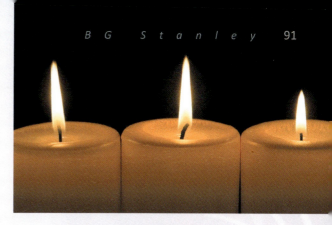

To my ancestors in Mother Africa:

Beautiful queen, noble king,
from your loins I came,
rich and royal, wise and brave,
never born to be enslaved.
The whole Congo was mine to claim,
the richness of the earth bore my name,
my body glowed like a glistening sun —
Yes, I was the 'chosen one.'

To my ancestors sold into slavery:

Because of you, I am strong.
Because of you, I can go on.
You sang my freedom song
before I even came along.
You sang for me that I would be free
from those who sold and captured thee.
From the Motherland you were taken,
abused, dishonored, but not 'God-forsaken.'

To the Civil Rights activists:

You were the ones who held the torch high,
You were the ones who made freedom cry,
You were the ones who marched, and died,
You were the ones America 'crucified,'
but you were the ones who rose again
to fight for justice for women and men.
You were the ones who continued to hope,
You were the knots at the end of the rope.
You were the ones who reached for the prize
that generations could continue to rise.
You were the ones who brought back
the dignity and pride of being Black.
With the Almighty behind you pushing you on
you challenged injustice, and you won!

And I am a branch that grows from the tree of these lives
in whom the spirit of Hope abides,
ingrained in a people determined and strong,
because of you, I can go on.

2006

My brother does not know me anymore

Separated   by a distant shore.
I was taken
he was left—
our faces are similar
but my brother does not recognize
that I have our Mother's eyes.
"You do not belong to me,
You were born in slavery,
You are not my Mother's child,
You are not my Mother's child."
But I want him to know and I want him to see
that I'm a part of him
and he's a part of me.
But my brother does not recognize,
I can see it in his eyes;
he speaks a language I used to know,
he lives in a culture I want to know;
I want him to be a brother to me
but he seems to be unable to see
that he is my family. . .
Separated at birth, now reunited,
a cause for jubilation—
but my brother says,
"you belong to another nation."
A nation forced to honor my life
forced to treat me like a man
forced to see me as a human being
took me from my own free land?
I, this stranger did not embrace,
I have my brother's rich dark face—
but, my brother says that I do not belong.
I do not belong . . . here . . . or there?

My   brother   does   not   know   me

              anymore.

tres Madres lloronanda (three mothers weeping)

Mother Mary wept because men took her innocent son and crucified him on Calvary.

Mother Earth wept because men uprooted her Native children and crushed their spirits.

Mother Africa wept because men took her sons and daughters and 'crucified' them in foreign lands.

Tres Madres weeping for their sons and daughters united in Spirit.

Three mothers weeping for their sons and daughters who through their suffering and oppression would bring liberation to both the oppressed and their oppressors.

For all the Black Women in the Struggle

For all the black women in the struggle
tenaciously fighting to unfurl dreams of justice and equity
making freedom a reality —
keeping homes together while supporting black men,
fighting injustice to the bitter end,
pushing their men forward, marching side by side
in solidarity, and loyalty, restoring their pride.
Black men, my brothers, open your eyes and see,
the progenitors, the pillars,
Black statues of liberty.
For black men alone could not have gained Civil Rights
without the sisters who stood with them
fighting the fight.

So for all the Black women in the struggle
We bear witness of you today,
We bear witness as we remember
the 'sistahs' who helped pave the way.

"Born Free"

No man gave me freedom.
I was born free.
No man could give me human rights,
they already belonged to me;
endowed by my Creator,
from the day the earth was formed,
no man could own my freedom,
'cause I was freedom born.

Free to be who I was
free to live and thrive,
free to walk upon this earth,
free to just survive.
But somehow in their confusion
men held others as slaves,
spat upon their humanity
because they were depraved.
    Too blind to see, too heartless to care,
    too dim to know, too selfish to share.
And so in truth my bondage
negated their liberty,
for those who held men captive
lost their own humanity,
until redemption came in 'Jesus' name,
and the Red Sea was parted again,
and those who held men captive
had to repent of their shameful sin.
They had to repent in order to know
the God of justice and grace,
for no one could claim to love God,
when they hated their brothers' face.
They could not see or know God
who sat with the despised,
they could not see or know God
until they opened up their eyes.
Opened their eyes to see their wrong
and relinquish their grasp on men,
until they acknowledged that slavery was wrong,
the greatest human sin.
And so the struggle for my freedom
and the struggle for equal rights
was won on the grounds of spirit and truth
because God was in the fight.
God was in the fight for human rights
for justice and equality,
God was in the fight for human rights
because God created all free.
Free to live; free to love;
free to simply survive,
God was in the fight because
injustice could not thrive
in a land where every woman and man,
every child and infant born,
was by nature of being flesh,
in truth and freedom formed.

No man gave me freedom.
I was born free.
No man could give me human rights,
they already belonged to me;
endowed by my Creator,
from the day the earth was formed,
no man could own my freedom,
'cause I was freedom born.

You Stood for US

(A litany)

Leader: You stood for us,

People: We *stand* because of you.

Leader: You sat for us,

People: We can *sit* because of you.

All: You *marched* for us,

bled and died for us,

went to jail for us

so that we could live free.

Leader: You dreamed . . .

All: And we can fulfill our dreams, because of you.

Waiting

In honor of the Civil Rights and Women Suffragettes
(For Dianne and me)

The lines were long
but we waited,
for 2 hours,
4 hours,
6hrs,
8 hrs
because you waited for days, weeks, months, years,
and marched,
and took the abuse.
So we waited for 8 hours to vote
because you waited even longer
just so that we could be able to wait.
    "Good things really do come to those who wait."

STANDING

What kind of man
Would ask a woman to stand
What kind of man
Could that be
On that bus
Who was he?
What kind of pride
Would make him want to ride
and sit
while a weary woman stood?
What kind of man,
what kind of man,
was he really a man
anyway?
She was already there,
already *sitting down,*
and she **STOOD** her ground,
they stood their ground,
and turned the world around.

Thank you Rosa,
Coretta, Dr. King, Lewis, Randolph, Farmer, Hamer, W. Young, A. Young, Abernathy, Sojourner, Dorothy Height, B. Hooks, Hosea, Rev. CT Vivian, H. Belafonte, Thurgood, Dr. Lafayette, Ella Baker, Nikki G., Angela Davis, Hank Aaron, Rev. C.L. Franklin, J. Chaney, A. Goodman, M. Schwerner, Wilkins, Lowery, JFK, Robert K., Maya, Bill, Marcus, Malcolm, Mandela, Chavez, Shuttlesworth, Jesse, Cooper, DuBois, Meager, Sharpton, Booker T., Bethune, Gandhi, Frederick, John Brown, Harriet; and every abolitionist, boycotter, Blacks and Whites, who **STOOD** for human rights.

Still STANDING.

THEY saw it Coming (A sermon revealed)

Martin dreamed of a day he saw coming.
From the mountaintop, he saw it coming.
Through the years, the rumbling of the ages;
from the Birmingham jail, he saw it coming,
on the streets of Alabama, he saw it coming.
All those marchers, Blacks and Whites, they saw it coming.
All those who sat at the counters defying discrimination with dignity,
they saw it coming.
All those who stood in the way of racism, and inequality,
and in the way of those dogs and hoses, and bats,
they saw it coming.
So they prepared a way, opened the doors
to the restaurants,
to the schools,
to the voting booths,
to every public place.
They had to clear some paths,
prune some trees of the disease of injustice,
turn over some tables of turmoil and unrest,
move some rocks and obstacles, jump some hurdles of hindrances,
weed out wrongs with swords of peace and truth.
They had to smooth some stony roads and lay some foundations.
They had to raise up some lowlands and low minds,
They had to dig some wells to quench their thirst
when they were denied a drink from the fountain of Liberty.
They had to adjust some unjust laws,
They had to cut out some old cancerous lesions in America, to make her better,
truer to her own creed.
They were clearing a path for all of us, for him —
brilliant, genuine, inclusive, ready, hopeful,
wanting better lives for every American —
seeking ways of peace,
so much like the dreamer;
different eras yet resounding themes of **CHANGE** and **HOPE.**
They cleared the path so that he could run
through the United States,
then walk, right into the White House.
They prepared the way,
While WE the People: Blacks, Whites, Asians, Latinos/Hispanics, and others
united fulfilling a common dream: the American dream, King's dream, his
dream, because,
THEY saw **him** coming.

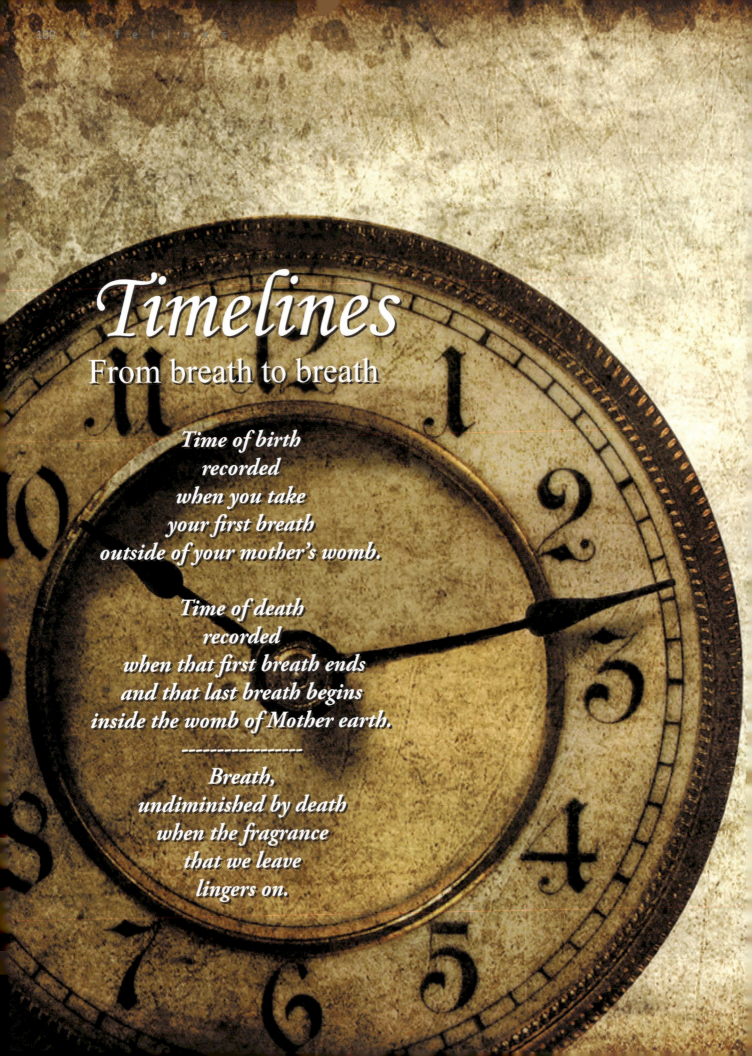

Timelines
From breath to breath

Time of birth
recorded
when you take
your first breath
outside of your mother's womb.

Time of death
recorded
when that first breath ends
and that last breath begins
inside the womb of Mother earth.

Breath,
undiminished by death
when the fragrance
that we leave
lingers on.

Kiss the Living

I wrote this poem in memory of my eldest sister, Dot, whom I will always love. I have many special memories of her as well a great respect and admiration. She was a strong phenomenal woman. From her I learned the true meaning of the transforming power of grace and forgiveness. She was so encouraging and supportive of my projects and ministry. She was a good mother to her children and grandchildren working hard and doing her best to ensure their happiness and success. I miss her dearly, but I catch glimpses of her in the faces of her children and grandchildren whom she deeply loved. My greatest comfort and joy is hearing her laughter inside my own.

Kiss the living,
not the dead,
say the words that should be said,
say, "I love you" in their ear
while they can know
while they can hear.
Say I'm sorry,
let's start again,
you may not get
that chance again.
So take the chance
to give peace
the chance to love,
the chance to reach,
while we live,
let's forgive,
wait not until someone
has passed away,
take the chance today
to
Kiss the living,
not the dead,
say the words,
that should be said,
say I love you,
in their ear,
while they can know,
while they can hear.

Kiss the living.

Save the Date

(In memory of my Dad, a great man amongst men).
This was my Dad's favorite poem. It speaks to his legacy. He spent a lot of time visiting the sick, the elderly, family, and making people laugh. He loved all of his family and was greatly valued and loved because he valued everyone. My dad was a charming man, a 'great soul.' He loved children and the elderly; people everywhere were drawn to him. My Dad was a masterful landscaper and arborist who employed and trained many young boys to become hard-working men. He was there for us as children and adults. He was a wise man from whom I learned so much. He was a great listener and a great conversationalist even with his slow mellow deep voice. When he heard this poem it struck a cord in him and he said, "read it again." He asked me to send him a copy so that he could pass them out because he thought that everyone should read it. He saw in it a greater meaning and understanding which made this poem even more special to me.

Plans are made from day to day
as we prepare for tomorrow,
not knowing if it will bring showers of joy,
or burdens of pain and sorrow.
We make plans for the holidays,
for weddings and festivities too,
but we should also make plans for the here and now
to do all the good we can do.
Let the date be today that you make someone smile
or take on a project, rewarding and worthwhile,
let the date be today that you celebrate your birth,
and tell someone how much they are worth.
Let today be the picnic, the dinner by candlelight,
let today be the family night.
Let today be the day to read that good book,
and finish the task you long forsook.
*Let the date be today that you make amends,
to love and enjoy your family and friends.
Let the date be today* to slow down your pace,
and take a moment to fully embrace,
memories and life, all the beauty to behold,
take time for the young, the sick and the old.
For tomorrow will come,
the next day and the rest,
but *let the date be today*
to give your all
and your best;
for next year,
you may not be here,
or a loved one may be gone,
so let each day be a special day
that your works of love live on.

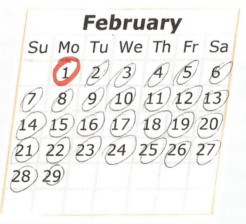

The living and the dead

Only one breath
separates life from death,
one heartbeat,
warm-cold,
a chasm;
a breath so long
we can sing a life song
and so narrow-
and fleeting;
gone too fast,
we wanted it to last.
We wish that we could
grasp
that breath,
that heartbeat,
and hold it
in our warm hands.

We wish that we could
give life to that silent heart,
but we can't!
Therefore, we live, laugh, and love
as much as we can
while we breathe
the same breath
on the same earth.

Love me now

I won't come to my funeral.
No, I won't be there;
so, if you got something to say, say it now,
'cause then, I won't care.
It won't matter if your words are splendid
and you say that you love me,
If you never told me while I was living
and never called me friend,
it won't matter then.
So many hours in a day,
but you had so little time,
now the hour you sit and mourn for me
is like fine broken wine.
Whatever flowers you have to give,
give to people while they live.
If there are things that hurt you
that someone may have done or said,
tell them while they are living
don't wait 'til they are dead.
Don't waste years being angry
over humanness, or simple mistakes
don't keep holding grudges
there are errors we all make.
Not one of us is perfect
not one without 'sin'
so learn to start from where you are
learn to begin again.
Learn to love while you can
Learn to give mercy and grace
Learn and strive to show kindness
while we live, face-to-face.
You may be surprised at what happens
if you give it one last try,
don't let the chance to make amends,
pass you right by.
You will miss out on good times together;
memories you'll forever keep,
so if you love me, show me now,
before I fall asleep.

My mother was an angel, a real gem.   She was profoundly brilliant, loving, kind, and caring for all of her children and everybody else's child.   She was so encouraging and helpful to so many people. At her funeral, someone said, she was like Mother Teresa. This was a true depiction of her life and her kind, gentle, giving spirit. We all have special memories of her. My last memorable moment with her was on my thirtieth birthday. She was hiding, waiting for me to come in from work. When I came in, she leaped out and started singing 'Happy Birthday'. She grabbed my hands and we started dancing around in the living room like two girls caught up in such a happy moment until my Dad came to the screen door peering in at us laughing. My mom had the sweetest spirit, a 'child-like' divinity.   On that day, I felt it so strongly that I said, Mom, you remind me of a little girl, but if I could only be one-fourth of the woman that you are. . .   I watched her and listened to her, now I strive to emulate her life and teachings. Oftentimes she would say to me, "Brim, I don't know what I would do without you," to which I would always respond, "No Mom, I don't know what I would do without you."

Mother – **[muhth-er]**

Even Webster's does not hold enough words to define
a mother.
Roget's synonyms are not enough to capture her heart,
her soul of gold.
Her touch; gentle hands that shape and mold.
No artist can fully paint the beauty of her face
nor capture the grace
in her eyes.
Her words, the sweetest melodies the ear will first hear.
Her love, wider than the world,
fathoms deeper than the deepest ocean,
open and limitless like the sky.
Yes, we can try,
but <u>infinity</u> and <u>divinity</u>
are the only two words that even come close
to the person who will always love you the most,
Mother.

Cemeteries

Cemeteries,
caverns holding the bodies of the dead
in solitude
underneath billowing trees
and blue skies that they no longer see,
flowers that they no longer smell,
sounds that they no longer hear,
not even the weeping of those
who come to visit and talk and pray
mourning the loss of their warm bodies,
the sound of their laughter,
the encouragement of their words,
the caress of their gentle hands,
the tightness of their hugs.
As I watch the cars passing by
I wonder if they know
who lies in the cemeteries?
I wonder if they know,
the 'specialness' of the names engraved on faded and new headstones.
I wonder if they pause to think about them
or wonder who they were from babies to centenarians,
once on earth,
now in the earth,
buried, but not forgotten,
for in the hearts of their loved ones they live on, —
memories unburied.
I wish that they knew my mother
like I did
and the richness that she brought to the earth that now holds her close,
but never closer than me.

Listen to her heart (Anamnesis)

In loving memory of the 'Queen,' my grandmother, May Francis Stanley.

Last year I was so excited about my grandmother's 100th birthday. I eagerly drove down to McRae to take her shopping to the mall in Dublin for a fancy green suit with a matching hat and purse. She was gorgeous. I spread the word about her upcoming birthday to my friends, co-workers, patients and doctors, and even the people in the store. One of the doctors said to me, "When you go to her birthday celebration, take your stethoscope and listen to her heart, and just think about how awesome, how profound it is; listening to a heart that has been beating for 100 years."

Well, I did take my stethoscope, and I did listen to her heart. As I was listening to her heart, I received a greater revelation. Listening to someone's heart is not merely a physical or mechanical entity. To listen to a heart whose rhythms of life express love and then to truly emulate that is what it means to listen to someone's heart.' I heard the rhythms of her life through my memories of her and from my relationship with this golden woman. I will never forget the letters she wrote me when I was a child, the old poetry book she gave me, the jokes she told me when I became a young woman and all of the births, birthdays, anniversaries, deaths, graduations, etc. that she remembered. I mostly enjoyed the stories she told me about the lives of our people as we rode down the country roads. One of my fondest memories is hearing her proudly recite her entire primer book from her early school years. She recited it several times and it was just as amazing each time. I had always marveled at her brilliance despite her never being able to complete school.

As I reflect on her life, and the person that she was, the rhythms that I have always heard were joy and laughter;rhythms of peace because she was always peaceable, promoting peace and togetherness;rhythms of love, because she loved all, deeply, unconditionally, especially her grandchildren;rhythms of giving, because she always gave so much of herself and whatever she had, (peanuts, quilts, preserves, peas, the list is endless);rhythms of forgiveness, as she shared with me how she had told all those who had wronged her that she forgave them, and was gracious enough to ask for forgiveness from anyone who felt that she had wronged them. I heard those heartbeats, those rhythms. They were the melody of a life well lived. Did you hear them too?

I cannot hear her physical heartbeat with my stethoscope now but I will always hear the rhythms of her life and stay in tune with the 'beating of her heart.' Lub-Dub, Lub-Dub; her heart 'beat' joy; her heart 'beat' peace; her heart 'beat' mercy; her heart 'beat,' giving, and these do not cease just as her love does not cease. Listen to the rhythms of her heart.

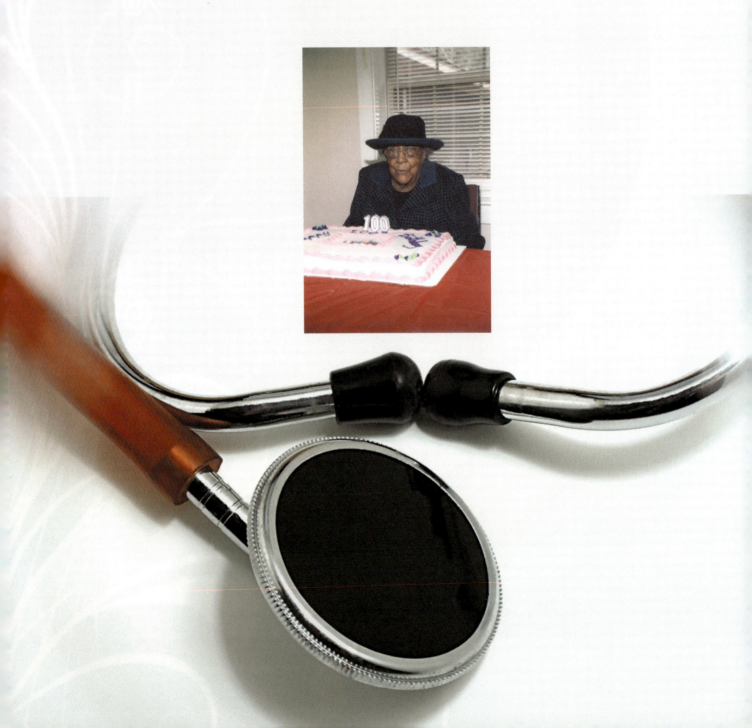

Images in order of Chapter/Source/Description/©Photographer/Collection

Image credits:

I. Connected:
> *Dreamstime-Unity and Strength/© Joseph Helfenberger*
> *Dreamstime-Fetus in womb/© Chrisharvey*

II. Breath of Life:
> *Dreamstime-Young beautiful woman praying in darkness/© Dmytro Konstantynov*
> *Dreamstime-Hands releasing bird into sun/© Norma Cornes*
> *Getty-Woman in water/David Mayenfisch/Workbook Stock*
> *Dreamstime-Free Soul© Karim Farah*
> *Dreamstime-Helping hands/ © Chaoss*
> *Dreamstime-Birthday Cake/© Wetnose 1*
> *Dreamstime-Sad teen girl/© Nikhil Gangavane*
> *Dreamstime-Ducks flying over calm lake at sunset/© Jaroslaw Grudzinski*
> *Dreamstime-Sticks and stones/© Georgios Kollidas*
> *Dreamstime-Precious girl holding candle/© Elena Volkova*
> *Dreamstime-Woman with red shawl walking away/ © Gopenshaw*
> *Dreamstime-Woman leaping high into the air/© Galina Barskaya*

III. Storylines:
> *Dreamstime-Once Upon a Time/© Connie Larsen*
> *Dreamstime-Silhouette of father holding children/© Sarah Nicholl*
> *istockphoto.com-Graduate/ © Edward Bock*
> *Dreamstime-Tied rope/© Hernan Pardo*
> *Fotosearch-mother and daughter embrace/Blend Images*
> *Dreamstime-Kite/© Alan Rodriguez*
> *Dreamstime-Woman at sunset/© Vasiliy Koval*
> *Skates and gold medal provided by Xlibris*

IV. Lifelines:
> *Jay Montgomery, illus., Woman pouring water on fruits, vegetables, fish, and grains*
> *Dreamstime-Bamboo trees/© Lidian Neeleman*
> *Dreamstime-Eagle/© Oliver Lenz*
> *Dreamstime-Lifesaver on pole/© Ron Chapple Studios*
> *Dreamstime-Hands holding key/© Olga Lyubkina*
> *Dreamstime-Senior woman wearing hat/© Justmeyo*

V. Children:
- *Fotosearch-Boy with red shirt/Blend Images*
- *Fotosearch-Boy holding dog/Blend images*
- *Fotosearch-Toddler kissing baby brother/Blend Images*
- *Dreamstime-little girl in pool*
- *Fotosearch-Little cowboys/Sassystock*
- *Vashun Bailey-Sharp boy in blue suit*
- *Fotosearch-Baby playing in leaves/Blend Images*
- *Mikai Jones-Sweet Sleeping baby*
- *Getty-Boys in sack race/Alstair Berg/Digital Vision*
- *Fotosearch-Children at computer/Blend Images*
- *Getty-Ballerinas/Tara Moore/The Image Bank*
- *Dreamstime-Round hut of the Ndebele tribe in South Africa*
- *Dreamstime-Little firefighter/© Geotrac*
- *Dreamstime-Little girl doctor/© Photoeuphoria*
- *Dreamstime-Young scientist/© Dgm007*
- *Dreamstime-Little boy in briefcase/© Photoeuphoria*
- *Fotosearch-Boy at board/Blend Images*
- *Dreamstime-Firefighter/© Monkeybusiness*
- *Getty-Female doctor looking at x-rays/Jon Feingersh/Blend Images*
- *Dreamstime-Scientist/© Forrest path*
- *Dreamstime-Business woman/© Petdcat*
- *Dreamstime-Math teacher at board/© Yuri Arcurs*
- *Banks and Spence Family Reunion in Lafayette, Alabama*

VI. Love lines
- *Getty-Loving elderly couple/Phil Borges/Stone*
- *Dreamstime-Doves with rings/© Svetlana Gucalo*
- *Dreamstime-Watering can and plant/© Alistar Cotton*
- *Curtis and Regina Anderson, Wedding Couple*

VII. Living Faith:
- *Dreamstime-Faith written in Stone/© Jill Lang*
- *Dreamstime-Moses/© Banilo Asciona*
- *Getty-Moses/Imaagno/Hulton Archive*
- *© Stephen Dalton-Brown Basilisk ('Jesus Christ Lizard') walking on water*
- *Dreamstime-Waters beating against rock/© Alexandr Tkachuk*
- *Dreamstime-Old Man walking/© Zagor*
- *Dreamstime-Silhouette of man praying/©Madartists*
- *Dreamstime-Violin/© Simon Jeade*
- *Dreamstime-Woman with outstretched arms/© Sergey Kravtsov*
- *Dreamstime-Ark of the Covenant/© James Steidl*
- *Dreamstime-Reflections/© Fotopitu*
- *Dreamstime-White boat/© Sean Nel*
- *Dreamstime-Lighthouse/ © Joe Mercier*
- *Dreamstime-The Climb/ © Bhairav*
- *Dreamstime-The Good Samaritan/© Yurly Nosenko*
- *Dreamstime-Cymbals/© xpdream*
- *Dreamstime-Gifts/© Mchudo*

VIII. Signs of Life:
> *Dreamstime-Pregnant woman © Vlavetal*
> *Dreamstime-EKG strip © Spectral-design*
> *Dreamstime-Ivy/© Miramisska*
> *Dreamstime-Mother and child signing I love you/© Sparkia*
> *Getty-Grandson whispering in grandfather's ear/Westend61/Westend61*

IX. The Magnificence of Life:
> *Dreamstime-Canyon Elbrus*
> *©John Lindsay-Edzell stained glass window/Permission to use obtained*

X. The Colors of America:
> *Dreamstime-World Map/© Btktan*
> *Dyson Giles-Handsome boy with black suit and tie*
> *Channel Marion-Little girl leaning on tree*
> *iStockphoto.com: Three friends smiling*
> *Getty-Teens with flags painted on faces/Tanya Constantine/Digital Vision*
> *Ta'Nae Tumbling-Baby doll looking girl with stuffed animal*
> *Fotosearch-Portrait of sister and brother/ "Unlisted Images, Inc."*
> *Dreamstime-Beautiful Asian woman with purple headress/© Maxfx*
> *iStockphoto-Girl wrapped in American flag/© Dieter Spear/Inhaus Creative*
> *Getty-Multiethnic American citizens waving flags/Jon Feingersh/Blended Images*
> *Dreamstime-Little African beauty/© Jennifer Russell*
> *Fotosearch-Baby maestro playing piano/"Unlisted Images, Inc."*
> *Getty-Hawaiian hula dancer/Turner and de Vries/The Image Bank*
> *Mikaela Anderson-Cute little girl in yellow dress*
> *Getty-Pretty girl looking over brick wall/Mark Hall/Stone*
> *Fotosearch-Young man walking with grandfather/Comstock Premium*
> *Ryan Cornish, Jr.-Baby boy reading book*
> *Getty-Little grads/Realistic Reflections/Realistic Reflections*
> *Maya Anderson-Cute girl with pink boa*
> *Tylin Jones-Handsome boy smiling*
> *Genesha Marion-Beautiful young lady wearing pink shirt*
> *Makenzie Anderson-Talented toddler in black Asian outfit*
> *Amari Jones, little boy holding toy car*
> *Getty-Children jumping together/Ariel Skelley/The Image Bank*
> *Jack and Suzanne Montgomery-Cute blonde brother and sister*
> *Kameron Nicholas-little boy wearing hat*
> *© Fleshtone rainbow created and designed by BG Stanley*

XI. Because of You:
> *Dreamstime- Man reaching for stars/© Marilyn Volan*
> *Dreamstime-Candles burning on black background/© Suljo*
> *Dreamstime-Oak tree/© Mahroch*
> *Andirka Symbol- "Never Forget" or "Return and get the lesson"*
> *Dreamstime-Pouring libations/ © Juliengrodin*

Dreamstime-Globe/© *Milosluz*
Dreamstime-Pieta/© *Szirtesi*
Dreamstime-Silhouette of Statute of Liberty/© *Kaarsten*
Dreamstime-Raised Hands/© *Dawn Hudson*
Dreamstime-Dream sky/© *Dmitry Maslov*
Dreamstime-Women's Suffrage Stamp/© *Sylvanna Rega*
Dreamstime-U.S. Election Voter's Hands/© *Madartists*
Dreamstime-Silhouettes of people waiting in line/© *Pavel Losevsky*

XII. Timelines: From Breath to Breath

Dreamstime-Vintage clock/ © *Sswartz*
Dreamstime-Three burning candles/© *Suljo*
Lawyer Stanley, Sr. (Dad) with granddaughter, Mikaela Anderson
Getty-Dana Spaeth/Pregnant mother and child/Photographers Choice
Dreamstime-Angel statue/© *Britishbeef*
Grandma May Francis Stanley at her 100th birthday celebration
Dreamstime-Stethoscope/© *Ed Isaacs*

ABOUT The Author:

BG Stanley was born and raised in Miami, Florida, and is the fourth child of eight born to the late Lawyer Stanley, Sr. and the late Lena (Montgomery) Stanley. Their love continues to be her constant strength and guide. BG Stanley was always an active member in church. She believes that her faith and spirituality has enhanced her appreciation and awe for life, people and nature. Stanley is a Registered Nurse and minister living in Georgia. After graduating from Miami Northwestern Senior High in Miami, Florida she attended Miami Dade Community College. She obtained a Nursing Degree from the University of Florida in Gainesville, Florida. She worked as a staff nurse on a surgical unit and in the Medical Intensive Unit at Jackson Memorial Hospital in Miami, Florida for many years before moving to Atlanta and working as a Surgical Intensive Care Nurse at Emory University Hospital. Stanley attended Candler School of Theology at Emory University earning a Master's of Divinity Degree in 2000. Her interests include teaching, writing, creating designs, listening to music, community service, improving race relations and spending time with her nieces and nephews who are the joys of her life. Stanley is the founder of 'The Colors of America' and Camp Diversity, a project dedicated to improving race relations by teaching children about different cultures and ethnic groups to promote acceptance, tolerance and a celebration of our own origins and diversity. Her inspiration for this project came from her participation in the Transforming Community project (TCP) at Emory University under the direction of Leslie Harris, Jody Usher, and Jyotsna Vanapalli. Stanley works as a volunteer with Partnership against Domestic Violence (PADV), and as a volunteer for Gwinnett County in Georgia. She is also a member of The Million Voices Campaign against domestic violence and abuse.

Her daily motto is to live life fully and allow others to do the same. True freedom lies in being able to express and be yourself with people who accept you and love you for your uniqueness. Life is about living 'your truths,' listening to others, and doing whatever good you can in this world.

CPSIA information can be obtained at www.ICGtesting.com
Printed in the USA
LVIW01n1136220817
545858LV00002B/3